The Mask I Wear

To Hide

The Pain I Bear

Justice Divine

Prologue

Those whose concern is for the victim as long as the perpetrator is not one of their own often defend the victim of sexual assault. The granddaughter and great-granddaughter following the funeral of another one of my relatives on Black Friday 2011 after she was informed that I was writing a memoir about my life sent the following message. The words are not devastating but indicative of the rules that have been embedded in many African American families: "what goes on in these four walls remains in these four walls." And those walls extend beyond the actual structure of a home but reside in the life of the child.

Abuses of all kinds become secrets due to the fear of taking the cover off the sin and saving the life of both the would would-be perpetrator and the victim. Fear is strong; when a life is in danger, they may be reluctant to talk about the fear. However, the effect balloons and the magnitude of caging it in for so long that one day like in

August 2010, their sacred Pandora's Box becomes too full and the lid bursts off. Death mattered not, nor did the protection of others; the only thing that lived was anger, unanswered questions, bitterness, and confusion. All actions were preceded with the very kind words of "you are so cute" until I began to think it was a curse. I began to understand that I was cursed as many others who are simply vulnerable, it is not about cute it was and remains to be about the opportunity to exploit ones vulnerabilities. When we fight back we risk losing our entire families, they do not rally but disperse as Peter did and other disciples when asked, "do you know this man?"; no one wants to be associated with the leper even if they become cured. Hush! They say, just let it go, look at what you have accomplished, and all you hear is Hush, don't tell nobody! If it hurts, just get over it and live but all you want is death because the lid will not fit back on the box.

Part I

The foundation of all things is the stabilizing force that causes the structure to stand or to fall! Deliberate or not the mind of all develops direction and patterns throughout childhood, the earlier patterns of behavior, values, beliefs and actions are embodied the stronger the life-long impact.

Chapter 1

When the passionate voice of inspiration
finds its true purpose, it will grow to a
mighty force that lifts the wings of change.
—Thomas Howard

Do you want to go play with the baby chickens, I heard him say. I saw an old house with a long dirt road, but no other kids were outside. He grabbed my little hand and we walked to the backyard where the chicken coup was. I looked at him and his face was brown with a burly beard and with a serious adult look, I did not know what any of it meant at the time. We continued to walk into the chicken coup and behind the wall that prevented a view from outside; we stopped, just short of the baby chickens. They were fluffy and yellow and were so small, I did want to hold one now that I saw them. When he stopped, he bent on one knee and took both of my hands in his as if to explain something. Allie I am going to let you hold one of the chicks but you have to be quiet or the momma hens will get you. I nodded my assent and he continued. Before I give you a special prize, you have to let me have a special prize, confused I said, "I don't have no prizes". He assured me that I had a very special prize and he would show me where it was, I nodded again. Looking at my face, he began to unfasten my shorts while reminding me to be very quiet. No thoughts came to me, at 4 years old; I did not know what was going to happen. He pulled them down with my panties, which were both, dirty from a week of wear. Looking intensely at my face he opened my legs and put his finger in my pee pee hole. Tears streamed down my face and he held one finger from the other hand to his lips for me to be silent. In and out, slowly in and out, in and out he continued and it hurt, but I just cried quietly and stood there. He then tried to insert two fingers and unconsciously I screamed in terror and quickly he pulled my shorts and panties up and ran with me out of the hen house. As he put me on the ground my mother opened the back door and asked what happened, he answered, "I guess she wanted to play with the biddies and the momma hen got after her". With a scowl, my mother spanked my bottom and said, "you will know next time not to mess with them chickens" and sent me to bed where I awoke next to my husband, as an adult unsure of the reality of the dream. Like all of the others it was so real, I felt the pain, I was there, and yet I awoke so far from 4 years old. Why do I have the nightmares?

Allie struggles to understand why her memories are so full of pain. The nightmares are worsening and her family is unsure of how to help with the painful dreams that negatively affect her rest. What actually happened, are the dreams real? If so, when did the terror began, why and by who? Allie rationalizes and researches the manifestations of nightmare and memories that seem too impossible to be true. Perplexed because all she finds is that they are subject to time and will, and often distorted. Maybe I am crazy; maybe what I remember is wrong. How do I find out, maybe hypnosis, or talking to someone; that will surely lead me to the confirmed crazy status. Now, I exist in a world where I am alone, scared, and ready to just die. These images frighten me and yet I must always smile, never cry, have it all together, education, style, body, conversation; no time to cry or talk about my fears or let them become known.

I hear different parts of me telling me what to wear, how to fix my hair, when to hide, when to eat, and when to purge. I listen, and the voices are not many but distinctive. For most of my life, others and I just thought I was erratic with my decisions, and it seemed true. Now, I hear the little girl who wants to play in the leaves, and the young girl who just wants me to do what I am told, and the teenager who is always angry, and the magician who vanishes without notice, and finally the smiling intellectual who speaks to thousands but cannot remember a single word. This is where I live and it is a terribly frightening place.

My escape is to do what I know well; give to others, so I will not be in trouble, this helps me to feel normal. I am obsessed with bringing my life into focus by searching for the lost puzzle pieces, but there are so many and my dreams couldn't possibly be real. Sacrifices seem to be redeeming, not freeing just redeeming. It is as if I can atone for what I do not understand but what controls my every decision and is very real in my actions. I am often informed that my friends, children and husband do not know who I am because of the erratic and different me's that arrive or change midstream. I do not know what that means, but I will find out.

I am Allie and this is I. I am caramel brown in the winter months and almond during the summer. I am 5'4" tall with a small build, dark hair that can fluctuate from being as curly as the top of a base cleft, to wavy as a perfect ocean with a slight breeze, or as straight as a stem of spaghetti before it is cooked. I am fit, I am anorexic, and I am alone with a wall so thick and tall that even the "Trojan Horse" cannot enter. You see I know I walk too fast, talk too fast, live in an all or nothing world, but what I do not know is why. Seeking to understand who I am and where I am from consumes much of my life. A broken past makes the future difficult to embrace. I need help and so I will share what I know and see if you can help me smile or cry and I know this is asking too much, but just to laugh freely. Not wear a mask to function in my daily roles, but for once have liberty. If you can, I am thankful and if you cannot I understand and still say thanks for trying. If you are lost, too maybe we can grow together as we try to understand.

CHAPTER 2

*In three words, I can sum up everything
I've learned about life: it goes on.*
—Robert Frost

Answers or Questions...

Allie poses the question to herself
knowing that the answer is unlikely to be
revealed. In her mind where she can be
honest, she thinks. I really think there is
a secret locked box that is within my soul
that holds all of the answers even the scary
ones. It sounds silly to say, but I have
seen it in my dreams. The box is in the
shape of an octagon with each of its eight
sides beautifully adorned in the vibrant
colors of the autumn season. Each side
appears to be perfect without defect. On the
aureolin side, the brightest color of them
all, there is a rusted keyhole resembling an
ancient entry point many centuries old. I
have seen keys that appear to be perfect in

local stores and pawnshops for years and yet not one of the long cross-shaped keys with various etchings and cutouts will fit.

This conundrum has brought me great stress and terrible nightmares where memories within the box strive to escape. The ambiguity of it all is so very overwhelming that I have gone to professionals who claim to have the keys to unlock the most challenging mysteries of the soul and for many years, I searched. I searched large cities, where professional counselors and therapist have degrees that cover entire walls, smaller cities where the best are known by all for their expertise, Christian, secular all experts. Not one in over thirty years could crack the lock. Often they were so captivated by the magnitude of the known memories and the personal accomplishments that they neglected to hear my need. Often their statements were "you have accomplished so much, do you believe it is wise to open up a box of painful memories"? I knew this statement was a sign to leave, for if I did not think it was wise, why would I be sitting before them asking for the very thing they question. I must find the key and I know God will lead me to the right person one day. I have to believe that I will not live in the darkness where there exist no demarcation from the beginning to the end and all is filled with miasma.

There are leaks in the box that are so tiny that I often find myself being accused of actions, or in the midst of conversations that leave me hiding in the closet shedding tears. Tears filled with lost time, space, actions and memory. I cannot dispute the accusations for too many corroborate them, but I do not understand why I have no memory. For years, sleep was hard to find and when it did reveal itself, it brought horrific nightmares and screams that were not heard. My prayer was always the same "God please let me stay sleep forever". It was too hard to manage the day and the night.

Allies' recall was limited to the tiny bits and pieces of life that often did not connect. She was left more confused because of their ambiguity and their lack of coherence. In secret, She asked the question "Am I crazy?" I have many names that have been poured on me and without clarity; I must accept them as truth. No one seems to answer my questions and many wonder why I cannot get past this curiosity and "let the past be the past". I am left feeling like a recluse in a crowd where only smiles are understood; therefore, I hide behind my smile. Everyone likes my smile "Allie you have a beautiful smile, one that brightens the world around you". I want to take off the smiling mask that eases the pain that others feel when one is deeply troubled. When it is, too much I go to the closet, sit in the dark corner, knees to chest, and cry alone until I can "get it together" and "put on a happy face".

This is my only protection, the only way not to reveal my brokenness and therefore I work diligently to live up to the expectations. Yet alone I continue to seek the best source to help unlock the cube. I do not know where to search thus I rely on God to show me the way that I must take. The elusive key prevents me from knowing who I am and where I have been so for me it is a treasure trove, and I must unlock, crush, or forget its existence.

This is not a literal cube that I could easily just crack open, take out all of the pieces, and put them together. No, it is held deep within the synapses of my brain and protected by the chambers of my heart, and known to me within my soul. It is unlike any deadly tumor you can imagine. It is not detectable with the greatest CT scan or MRI and certainly, no simple X-ray could find it. Yet, I know it is there and it must be opened gently and its contents must be handled with care, for they have aged as if they were part of a great collection of medieval artifacts found in the crevices of Mesopotamia.

Although modern machinery cannot find this box to operate and remove it, it has begun to leak and those closest to me are afraid, they watch their words, walk on eggshells and whisper so that I do not react inappropriately. The slippage that pours through its cracks in the form of tears that are not understood, or anger that arises to avenge a wrong that is partially remembered, or a fall back into a lost child who must obey or miss food, get beaten, locked away, worked, raped, drugged, sodomized and no one understands; not even me. I just become a person who must "get over it" before it drives me crazy—too late. These atrocities are woven into my body and are true memories; but I am confused as to how they came to be. What did I do to be banned from eating, locked in an attic as enslaved 7-year-old worker? The energy that it takes for me to manage the memories is often overwhelming and unbearable, therefore, I am learning to think about it in small doses. This has yet to be mastered, but sanity warrants it, life warrants it, and without it, I will not live.

CHAPTER 3

Reality continues to ruin my life.
—Bill Watterson

Two years after the fingers the cube
was formed. This time Alison could not run.
No please don't please I don't want to
go nooo stop get off it hurts please it
hurts I'm sorry please let me go I
don't want to, please give me my
clothes, ….I hear them saying shut up,
if anybody hears you, you will get a
whooping, and next time I bet you will
shut up, are you ready to for your
turn, I will hold her and she better
shut up before I hit her, Ough that
hurts, it hurts please. I like the tree
and will not come from the tree, she
cries, I will read and help her not to
cry anymore or scream let's just read
about Laura in the big woods she Is our
favorite you can be here now and we can

sit and go on an adventure, don't go

back don't go back it hurts don't ever

go back this is our secret, no one will

know we are Laura.

Laura arrived in time to make the pain stop.

I went on adventures, went to school with my

books tied with a string and Ma and Pa told

me to go straight to school. I liked school

but that Nellie always had the best stuff

cause her Ma and Pa owned the General store.

Somehow, I realize that I am not Laura

but Alison and I am now lying on the ground

naked and in pain. Tears are streaming and

my clothes are next to me. I am not sure

what happened, I remember begging and

screaming for them to stop hurting me, I

could not run like I did with the fingers,

and the pain cannot be accurately explained.

Box without Keys

Boxes had been constructed for many

generations before the construction of my

box; but because of the refusal of past
generations to find the key I became a
member of the Box Heritage. For many
generations sexual assault including rape,
incest, sodomy, human trafficking and other
atrocities has been a part of human culture.
This is supported by research into the
history of sexual assault conducted by Donna
Macnamara (2005).

> Understanding the history of sexual
> violence and the social and political
> functions that it serves can go a long
> way in helping us facilitate healing
> with individuals and inform our work in
> public education and systems change.
> This is particularly critical when
> working with people of non-European
> descent. By breaking the silence about
> the long history of systematic cultural
> genocide and the many abuses that
> occurred throughout history, we give
> permission to our clients to break
> silence about their abuse and we are
> able to maintain a clear understanding
> of the importance of systems and social
> change.

> Construction began with the foundation
of the earth filled with humans who learned

by their struggles, fears, refusal of rights, bondage, beatings and the cold non-feeling way of engaging in atrocities where they could not explain or even acknowledge the horrible pain they endured. The only way to escape is to become someone else, or to become what you endured. As one who loved to read, I became someone or many others to escape my reality. As life was filled with repeated sexual assault and exploitation, I became many people from childhood to adulthood. The pornography, beatings, pain and sodomy were unbearable therefore; the box became my "Black's Box" and all unbearable experiences were stuffed into the tiny opening. The entry point was a slither similar to the opening on a child's beloved "piggy bank", just large enough to let them glide from my consciousness and into the box without a key, to be buried forever. I did not know how to help the girl that looked like me. I heard her cries and watched what was happening to the poor girl, but I was too afraid to stay and I went far away and hid in the tree.

I was happy because I found myself living the life of Laura Ingalls from the Little House on the Prairie series. I had on a dress with a petticoat with black boot shoes running to school. I ran as fast as I could until I tripped and fell hard on the ground waking to see and feel my reality. Laural often found herself in puzzling situations but she always landed in the safe and protected arms of "Ma and Pa". I landed on the hard ground with nothing covering my body or anyone tending to my injuries. Alone, scared, hurting I used the box without a key to get rid of the monstrous experience. I could not make sense of it and would rather believe it never occurred.

However, as time progressed I remember
having to revisit the box to add other
painful experiences. Life gave no time to
wander what caused the pain, only time to
put it away and get back to the current
state of mind that must remain rational at
all times. Rape, words, touches, punches,
slaps, all added many times over 15 years.
Loneliness was thrown in the box, realizing
that focusing on living without stability
was what my life would be and to feed the
feeling would not change the circumstance;
another feeling in the box. The wall around
me is getting higher to protect my heart and
mind from my reality. I wanted to forget
that this was living because I realized that
false hope would get in the way of
performance. Blocking feelings yielded a
robotic disposition. That included
developing a smile that was welcoming, a
voice that was inviting and body language

that responded appropriately. I left this world and hoped the reality would be forever in the recesses of my brain but not come to my frontal lobe and be recalled by my long-term memory.

I guess there really is not much difference in the semantics of what you call it, it just had to all go away, and the box was the only place to put it where no one would see or know how I could survive with such a large and ever growing box hidden within. Many do not survive with just the smallest part of what is in the box, but I was brilliant, I made it undetectable and learned how to be what I needed to be to prevent the reality from taking hold of me. I would immediately stuff it into the box and put on the right face to live in the moment. It worked and was my first tactic to coping with reality; my second was to build a wall so high and thick that no one could get close enough to know what or who was really behind the impenetrable construction.

For me the thought of others knowing the things that were placed in the box or seeing the stains on my flesh left an indelible fear in my cognition that I would be attached to such descriptors like slut, whore, prostitute, fast, and worst of all trash. Now, do not get it confused I knew that I was each of these descriptors. My only confusion was that I never asked, consented or freely engaged in the tragic abuses. My screams were silent, my pain was stuffed away, and tears were only present when there was a closet to hide in. Silence was beat into me from the very first time. "Go clean your face up and go back outside and play, this is life and you better not tell anyone or you will get a whipping," my mother's words rang loud and true. I learned that silence prevented only a modicum of pain, but with so much pain, having a little

peace would have been a precious gift.

CHAPTER 4

To live is the rarest thing in the world. Most people exist, that is all.
—Oscar Wilde

Choosing Silence

Yes, I chose silence, forced to be there in body but learned to find somewhere else to be in mind. The only way to exist was without connections, relationships, home, morality and anything that would interfere with being perfect in the moment. By wearing a mask and playing the role, that I was charged with, I am alive. This was not my choice for 15 years I prayed daily to die, I tried to leave permanently but the pills never worked. I believed that when I was sleep I had peace and if I could just sleep forever all pain would go away. It is obvious that my attempts were futile.

I never thought about the mind, what was its relevance. It worked because I could put on many faces and characters to survive, and just place the reality in the box. Many say because I put this pain in words, "she just wants attention at other people's expense." I hoped my invisibility would help me to avoid attention, but I do want to draw attention to the voices that are silenced and taking Prozac, Xanax, Lithium and other psychotropic drugs to deceive the brain. Manufactured happiness to counter the Man-who-fractured where the happiness that existed. The development of a powerful industry to provide medications for "happy" and medications to "forget" the fractured and often brokenness that consumes every moment as the pressurized box has fully expanded and suddenly burst. Yes, often called "crazy, full of demons, off her rocker, mixed up in the head", and an array of other terms to explain actions that are revealed when there is no more room in the box, and the victim "cracks" into a million small pieces.

Abuse does not end when the act is over, it never ends, and this book is to give voice, hope, and freedom to others who have experienced forced physical, emotional and psychological abuse that leaves behind hopelessness, loneliness, and worthlessness. We cannot change yesterday but we must find a way to start living in the present therefore, I share my box that burst just prior to my 40th birthday, but had leaked for many years. The patches that I used were raising children, trying to be a good wife, and education but eventually the children were raised and school was complete, while the marriage was fighting to hold onto the slippery edge that the cracked box pushed me over. The intimate details of my life are without regret, I cannot remain a victim and I cannot scream, but I can write, I pray this method helps to empower those who want to know that through it all God is there, even when it seemed like he hated me by letting me be brutalized and traumatized for 15 years. I know judgment will come, but I am not writing to those who will curse the very idea of putting my experiences into words, criticize my mistakes, accuse me of "wanting" or "deserving" what I received, and angry at themselves for not yet being ready to be free. My greatest prayer was for God to protect my daughters' and help me not to perpetuate the cycle of abuse and now that they are grown, I can praise him for hearing my prayer.

Part II

THE MASKS THAT I WEAR PROTECT ME FROM THE
BEING REVEALED, THE EDUCATION AND FAMILY
WERE BOTH TO HELP WASH MY FILTH AWAY, BUT
THE DUST THAT I AM REMAINED INTACT AND
THE CONSTANT REMINDERS FROM THOSE WHO SAY
"I REMEMBER WHEN…." KEEPS ME HIDING
BEHIND A SMILING FACE JUST TO EASE THE
PAIN. NOT WORTHY TO BE DIRT, DUST IS ALL
I AM AND I AM AFRAID TO REMOVE IT
COMPLETELY, BUT IT IS TIME.

CHAPTER 5

I'm the one that's got to die when it's
time for me to die, so let me live my life
the way I want to.
—Jimi Hendrix

Present Day

Looking at me today, you would see a forty-two-year-old, 5'4" tall woman with a delightful expression for the public and if possible, the reconstruction of my mind as I strive to face the monsters of my past. You would consider that all was well and if you knew me, you could not imagine why I complain, and like others, you may say "girl you gotta let that stuff go, look at where you are now. Shoot if I had what you have I would say forget that mess and live and enjoy my life". If I could make the movie stop running in my head, reminding me of the terror of life before, I would and I am learning to see myself the way God sees me and that is with tender, nurturing love. I believe that I am closer than ever and one day I will Love Me the way He loves me.

You see I am the face of Black women everywhere, those that are deeply pained and visually upwardly mobile. However, the internal struggle to gain personal ownership of our bodies, intelligence, and the height of our ceilings is yet to be realized. Thomas Thistlewood, the young man from Lincolnshire who settled in Westmoreland Parish, Jamaica in 1750 is one of the most recognized barbarians of slaves and Black women in particular. Black women for centuries have been the property of others sexually, physically, and emotionally. For example in *Mastery, Tyranny, and Desire: Thomas Thistlewood and His Slaves in the Anglo Jamaican World (Burnard, 2004)* writes "for Thistlewood, as well as for many other white men in Jamaica, sex with enslaved (black) women was an important strategy to prove the **dominance of master over slave"**. Burnard (2004) also states that, "the institutional dominance of white men had to be translated into personal dominance" (p. 160) and that is achieved by personal degradation, power, and the threat/reality of being brutalized.

No, I am not known throughout the world or the United States of America, and for that matter not even in my local community but my experiences do reflect those of many women throughout the world, yet the face in the mirror is a black face. This black face is taking off the mask that allowed my limited existence. You see I exist in the realm of personal accomplishment and limited publicity not because I am so great, but actually, because I lack the confidence to think of myself outside of the events of my life. Sounds narcissistic, but no there is no room to think the world revolves around me, just the opposite; I do not belong in this world.

To be transparent, as of today I have been married to a man most call a saint for nearly twenty-one years and have two honorable and cherished daughters. I have three college degrees: a BA, MS, and PhD and I have been recognized for providing college access to marginalized youth. I have been a gateway for many to empty their struggles in my lap and a voice of reasoning to help them through the next moment, hour, day, or week. All of this is merely the surface of what you will hear and see if you knew me and because the surface is what many see, the depth of my brokenness seems unfounded. Thanks to the smile that hides the sadness and the mask that dries the tears, I am living in a cloud of miasma that I never seem to leave behind.

For twenty-three years, I made a life that suited the Bible, my family and the community. Alison lived for everyone as she always had without the abuse, but she maintained a life that kept her fully occupied like that of Martha trying to prepare for Jesus until he said sit and listen (Luke 10: 38-41):

> "[38] As Jesus and his disciples were on their way, he came to a village where a woman named Martha opened her home to him. [39] She had a sister called Mary, who sat at the Lord's feet listening to what he said.
> [40] But Martha was distracted by all the preparations that had to be made. She came to him and asked, "Lord, don't you care that my sister has left me to do the work by myself? Tell her to help me!"
> [41] "Martha, Martha," the Lord answered, "you are worried and upset about many things, [42] but few things are needed—or indeed only one.[f] Mary has chosen what is better, and it will not be taken away from her."

I busied myself trying to be a good wife to my husband and an excellent mother to my daughters, for I could not fail at this task. Additionally, education was necessary in an attempt to wash away the filth that I was known for and to help divert the attention away from my feeling of nothingness. Yes, I was the quintessential mom at the school programs, ensuring that my daughters had equal access to all that was available. I was the mom who prepared dinner and insisted on everyone eating together in the kitchen without external noise. Dinner was about catching up on the day's events, including work and school, giving nuggets of wisdom and insisting on appropriate etiquette. No, it was not wrong but the reasons were misplaced, making failure appear to be looming and one mistake would destroy it all. Living in a world that I had not been prepared for (mother and wife) caused great anxiety for there were no directions, and there had been no example, making failure highly probable.

Working in a job where I was legally paid began at the age of 14 and thankfully continues. I worked many jobs in federal, state, corporate, nonprofit, education and retail while always attending school full-time and refusing to get less than an A in every class. Of course, frustration set in when the A was just impossible (Spanish) so the C was graciously accepted. Keeping my mind occupied with school and legitimate work made the world of forced labor easy to dismiss. Disconnecting from the abuses was the only way to excel in the other areas.

I put that work ethic into my girls as if their very lives depended upon their excellence. They were taught that they were geniuses from conception and nothing but excellence in all areas was acceptable. They grew up with my most famous words being "suck it up" and "unacceptable behavior" because I was working so hard to have worth and they would have it even if I did not know how to give it to them, they would not be dirt. The pressure for them to succeed so that I could have a check mark in my column nearly caused them to feel that the bar I had was unreachable. I could not see that I was pushing too hard, but I am blessed with a husband that could balance my unyielding requirements with sensibility. My consumption with wanting to be "good" at something superseded those that were the objects of my "good". I continue to regret my actions, not because our girls are not wonderful, but because I only remember doing and not being.

At twenty-three and nineteen they are their own masters, one completing graduate school elite ivies, and the other attending one of the nation's top universities. I am proud, but I did not know how to teach them anything but survival. How to cook, manage disappointments, expect disappointments from everyone, ignore pain, love was a myth, being attractive was a magnet for trouble, and affection, well I did not know how to do that, therefore I hugged them when they cried, or if they seemed sad because that is all I wanted; just a gentle caring hug.

   My longsuffering husband has a story of his own that he will share. I am sure it will differ greatly because perspective becomes truth and the prescription lenses that he is embedded with are quite the opposite of mine. I can with much assurance state that it was not an easy journey building a marriage on quick sand, yet for many years we did. Living with a wife who had so little to give but whose needs were greater to bear than a toddler learning to

walk by trying to climb Mt. Everest. To
this, I must say he continues, often times
blindsided by my personal and unexplainable
struggles, to remain deeply and forgivingly
in love with me.

CHAPTER 6

Tiger mothers are strict parents who demand excellence in academics from their children. "The Tiger, the living symbol of strength and power, generally inspires fear and respect.
—Amy Chua, Battle Hymn of the Tiger Mother (2011)

Failing While Trying to Succeed

I glaze over the surface of the twenty years because I lived them as a task to be accomplished and checked off my "to do list." Therefore, the details seemed irrelevant. It was not until 2007 where the details were all that mattered. Not until the week after Thanksgiving 2011, did I start therapy. I was placed on strong medications to minimize suicidal actions, control anorexia and prevent night terrors. Like so many, I hated the medicine and the way it made me feel, I constantly felt nothing, and slept, and continued to refuse to eat. Pain unlike any I had ever felt would not go away, I could not find my mask, and I had no more busy, I just wanted to die.

In the summer of 2007, my oldest daughter was preparing to enter her senior year in high school while my youngest was preparing for the 8th grade, her last year in middle grades. I was intent on making sure my oldest had a head start on preparing for college, not her interest but mine. I forced her to complete her college applications, essays and all other college admissions work prior to the actual school year beginning. I had the scholarships organized the essay topics ready and although the applications would not be available until August, she was to complete all of the task required by the state college application portal so that on that day August 1, 2007 we could upload documents, essays, and personal statements and submit applications. Again, completing another task to check off the lists I created in my mind of being a good parent.

She was miserable and agitated and rightfully so, because I was relentless, nothing else mattered except getting her applications submitted and applying for all scholarships available to her. I did not see myself as over bearing or insensitive or just mean, I was being a "good mother" I had prayed everyday not to fail at this most important job, but I had no experience and worked on instinct, not feelings. I had become consumed with her life to the point that she was miserable, we were at odds most of the summer and throughout the year. She complied with all of my edicts, including one that brought her to great tears, but did I stop. No, my life was a failure and it was my responsibility to make sure that I did not hurt my children or allow them to fail.

They had been successful and would always be successful.

I insisted that she break the two-year relationship she had with her boyfriend and informed them both that it would end immediately after graduation because they would go their separate ways. He to his university and she to hers, I made sure they would not be at the same institution. She was angry and throughout this time, her sister and my husband were feeling the force of my push on her future. I had her apply to the summer preparation program at her future institution so that she could get a head start and not have access to her "high school friends" the summer before college and of course, she was admitted. The day her acceptance into the program arrived, she fell into deep despair with tears like a river flowing after a category five hurricane. I tried to console her and refused to let her feel even that pain. I forced her and my family to go out for dinner with the hope that it would alleviate her pain.

I recognize that it was not her pain that I worried about it was that she would not be disappointed in my decision. She did not cry but she did not laugh either, the program started on the day of her graduation, which meant that she left the ceremony and went straight to the campus to move in with a stranger. She had no time to reflect on her accomplishments, say goodbye to friends, or have dinner with all the guests who came to celebrate her moment of success. In preparation for this quick move, I planned her family celebration for the day before and orchestrated her life like it was not hers but mine. Throughout the entire year, I was too busy to care and to busy not to care. Too busy to focus on what my actions were doing to her, and to busy thinking and worrying about what others may say if she was not perfect.

Simultaneously, my younger daughter was seeking admission into the elite boarding high school for juniors and seniors. Again, I insisted that she take the highest level of courses available in the district and required her to take the standardized test beginning in 7th grade. I lacked compassion when her most important class had problems with securing a teacher, I required her to learn independently, with our help or with a tutor, and nothing less would be acceptable.

No excuses were allowed. I was alienating my husband believing that he did not support me and never had. My girls were miserable, everyone was walking on eggshells, and I could not see why there was so much confusion. I cried, but did not know why, our home was no longer a place of peace, but a place where confusion, anger, regrets, and loneliness resided. I Alison Sloan had lost control and now my family was suffering because of me, my only hope was to remove myself from the picture.

CHAPTER 7

*The most terrible poverty is loneliness
and the feeling of being unloved.*
—Mother Teresa

Lonely, but not Alone

Soon I realized that I was consumed with the fear of my child leaving me. The one I had that was supposed to love me forever and never leave was doing just that, leaving. I know rationally, that it was the natural progression of life, but the circumstances of her coming to be were not rational. At eighteen years of age after graduating from high school and attending a large urban university for only a few months before withdrawing, I felt so lost and alone that I wanted to have someone that would always be with me and love me unconditionally. I did not want a husband or a boyfriend, but a baby. I told my boyfriend at the time that I wanted a baby.

Astonished, and against his moral judgment he consented; and in October of 1989, I conceived just as I turned nineteen years of age.

Oh, I was elated, he loved me enough and wanted to do the honorable thing and get married, but no way was I going to share my child with anyone. My aunt and no one else could understand my decision to go solo on having a child when I had such a great person who wanted to take me as his wife and we raise our child together. "No one is going to want a ready-made family" was my aunt's retort; of course, I ignored those words and the wishes of my ex-boyfriend. I knew that this was my jewel and no one would have a piece of her but me.

In February of 1990, I sold my furniture and bought a one-way ticket to Virginia without telling anyone. Although I was not allowed to move into my mother's home, I did not despair because I had been alone all of my life and I expected nothing from her. I did get an apartment and a job working at a common fast food eatery from February 1990 throughout my pregnancy. I never once considered calling her father or others to inform them of my whereabouts. I wrote my unborn child a letter on April 29, 1990:

To my unborn child:

I've adored you since you were conceived. Most expectant mothers' go through all sorts of changes, but you didn't once make me sick. I cried many nights while carrying you because I felt so lonely. Once you started moving on the inside, I began to really feel your presence. I am now anxious to

hold you, to play with you, and
most importantly to love you.
Love,
Mommy!
April 29, 1990 at 8:27 PM

A month later on June 1, 1990, I wrote a "poem" to myself hoping for comfort as I waited on her to arrive.

The Ultimate Test

There are often times when life seems
to stand still
Times when our patience is put to the
ultimate test
More often than not we fail such a
test.
Test that are very simple to pass to
those looking in, but, test that are very
difficult to those on the inside. Yet, once
we're on the outside we seem to
easily forget.

We forget about the seconds we watched tick by.

Once we see another holding the same position we remember slightly; but never to the extent that not so long ago wasn't a memory, but, the ultimate test of our patience.

June 1, 1990

This was my child and she was going to love me forever and never leave. Two weeks past her due date of May 28th she was born on June 14 1990. I felt every emotion possible holding her and knowing that my life would never be the same.

CHAPTER 8

*There comes a point in your life when
you realize who really matters, who
never did, and who always will.*
—Unknown

The End before the Beginning

Like many girls who are thrown away, I
expected nothing from the world and had too
much pride to ask for help. My older sister,
and younger brother and even my mother
helped me after she was born. However, she
was indeed mine and I did not want to share
her with anyone.

Then one day in August, I began to hear
voices and hallucinate. The man's voice
suggested that I was incapable of being a
good mother, I was not good enough to take
care of my daughter and she would be better
off with someone else, anyone else other
than me. I fought to stop the voices but
they continued to trouble me in my waking
and slumber hours. I would turn the man's

deep voice off because it seemed to be coming from the television, then it would come from the small radio that played on the counter, so I would turn it off. I continued to hear the man's voice say, "your life is not worth living, you should just die and make the world better for everyone especially your child. She is doomed with you as a mother, what can you offer her."

Call me crazy, the voices were loud and for me at that time just as real as my own voice. The third week of August after being in the apartment for the obligatory six weeks and having sparse visitors except my older sister who visited daily after work, I sat alone with this perfectly beautiful child. She did not cry much she was perfect but all I saw was my imperfection and all I could hear was the voice of a man that would not shut up telling me that I would destroy her chances if I did not kill myself.

Finally, I relented and decided that with my history and destructive past, the man was right and I would try only one more thing before my eyes would close for good. There was no faith, no belief of any kind that this last ditch effort would work, but I tried anyway. With so much sincerity and conviction I said, "God, I am going to give you one chance to make my life right, so I am going to go to church tomorrow, even though I don't believe in church, but if you don't fix my life tomorrow I will come home and take these pills and die." I had a bottle of prescribed pain pills that I poured out next to my bed and mixed them with other over the counter medication, not believing for one second that I would live past that Sunday.

PART III

IT IS NATURAL THOUGHT TO BELIEVE THAT
ONE KNOWS THEIR JOURNEY, THAT THEY HAVE
BEEN PRIVY TO EACH STEP AND A PART OF
EACH DECISION. MY JOURNEY IS ONE THAT
HAS ONLY PARTIALLY BEEN REVEALED, FOR I
WAS NOT A PART OF THE PLANNING ONLY A
PARTICIPANT OBSERVER WITH NO POWER TO
START OR TO END. THE JOURNEY WAS SET
BEFORE I KNEW MY NAME AND WHAT I KNOW
COMES FROM THE EXPLOSION OF THE BOX,
JAGGED MEMORIES, VARIOUS FORMS OF
THERAPY AND NIGHT TERRORS.

CHAPTER 9

When I hear somebody sigh, "Life is hard," I am always tempted to ask, "Compared to what?"
—Sydney J. Harris

In the Beginning . . .

Hiding behind a smiling face was the best protection I had from all who would ask, "What is wrong". However, even the greatest brightest smile cannot be hidden behind soulless eyes, without love, hate, or satisfaction could be seen; just the emptiness of eyes that looked past the pain.

Twenty years have passed and many schemes have been tried to maintain the mask, smiles no longer were effective and oftentimes refused to be visible. The hurt that came each time I realized I was no ones, the loss of purity that so many remember giving in love and most importantly the stains of filth that was left behind

were all hindrances to gaining freedom. I
knew I would never be free, the hurt was
deep in my soul, the innocence once lost
could never be returned and the filth was so
deep that removing the outer layer of my
epidermis could not cleanse me; therefore,
my soul was lost in the cesspool of a world
that did not need or want my presence.

Allie's future was set at the early age
of four, as she played alone outside,
molested by the common perpetrator her
"uncle" and scolded by her mother her
destiny was written and would be fulfilled.
The beginning was a mystery for a long time,
the incident to fill in the holes of my
empty life I asked others' about partial
memories and created a white washed past
from their answers. Now, that I have
crashed and landed at the bottom of the all
I think about is how to live no more. "Do
you think about suicide asked my therapist"

it is all I have thought about for 40 years and now I get pills to numb me and return me to a soulless existence.

Allie has been forced into therapy for the 10th time since childhood, but it is the first time she believes it is necessary. Therapy happened and I opened myself up to anything that was to help me find my way to a place I have not known for 40 years, back to Alison. I liked the therapist who chose a form of therapy referred to as EMDR or Eye Movement Desensitization and Reprocessing (EMDR) a "comprehensive, integrative psychotherapy approach". She explained that this approach might have an immediate positive effect. "It contains elements of "many effective psychotherapies in structured protocols that are designed to maximize treatment effects". Of course her words were gibberish to me but I was in no position to make a decision. Per Mrs.

Barbara EMDR includes psychodynamic, cognitive behavioral, interpersonal, experiential, and body-centered therapies."

The pamphlet she provided from the EMDR Institute, Inc. states: "EMDR psychotherapy is an information processing therapy and uses a structured approach to address experiential contributors of a wide range of pathologies. It attends to the past experiences that have set the groundwork for pathology, the current situations that trigger dysfunctional emotions, beliefs and sensations, and the positive experience needed to enhance future adaptive behaviors and mental health."

Opening me up to therapy for the first time was scary, the thought of remembering how my life ended up here was not a welcoming thought but a journey that I could no longer ignore. She began with simply talking and getting an overview of what I recalled and after a few weeks I was informed that I suffered from Post-Traumatic Stress Disorder (PTSD) and Dissociative Identity Disorder (DID. She explained that the diagnoses resulted in unexplained lost time and space, angry outburst and unusual actions that could be triggered daily or single encounters. I am aware that I was non-confrontational and would rather deal with challenges by pushing them in the box or leaving the scene and living in my head, therefore to be at the brink of resurrected what I feared consumed reactivated my fight or flight button.

Today, I cry, tears so full of pain that I would love to run, yet I do not I go to therapy and follow it with a different escaping mechanism that I had avoided all of my life. A simple glass of Merlot with two anti-depressants and two prescribed sleep aids work wonders. The alcohol I drank to drown my emotions in did not help but adding the soulless medication was perfect. It prevented the night terrors and the visions that were discussed during the sessions, sure, it is not good, but what has been?

Along the journey I decided to search for my true beginning, my birth certificate is useless; it is filled with all incomplete or wrong information. I located school documents and medical records that helped to identify some of my locations, which narrowed down the pool of perpetrators including father, brothers, uncles, ministers, deacons, strangers who paid, and strangers who took. After a while, I did not see their faces or feel their slaps, kicks, punches, or extension cords, sticks, cameras, or gazes. I just knew they were there. Not because of the drugs, I was forced to consume, but because of the overwhelming trauma that followed each hit and by the lingering bruise, bloody back filled with whelps or simply finding myself hiding in the woods, in a closet or behind a dumpster. Each scar was followed by a physical scar that had to scab over or the throws of hunger that left me dazed and unable cognitively to think and worst the emotional scars that yearn for my life.

The drugs that I do not know the names of were to make me less aggressive and more malleable; the beatings were to reveal the power that the owner/perpetrator had over me to reach the same outcome through physical aggression. Just as my ancestors who were constantly being sold as property, I faced the unfortunate destiny of living at a time when this was illegal but not challenged. The result of me constantly running away, believing there must be something better, seeking safety from pain, but mostly trying to find ways to ignore the memories of the past hurts with the belief that it would magically be forgotten if I could ever find safety.

Yet here I am sitting alone in this place taking Prozac to be happy and Klonopin to prevent feelings from surfacing and Trazodone to sleep. Am I living yet or just existing? True and false fears or anxiety that cause my heart feel like it will jump through my chest at any moment if I do not *run*, just run. During the actual abuse I could simply go away and feel nothing, now I am completely powerless as I am forced by time to relive it so many years later. The images and movies that play behind the screens of my eyes where rest should reside, cause night sweats, fear, screaming and worst of all they cause me not to recognize my location, family or my current station in life. I do not want to watch the movies but when the curtains close, the pause button is released, and the play button is depressed.

As a little girl I had this all figured out, and for so many years, disappearing when the hurt came, worked perfectly. I mastered the art of only revealing what was necessary to maintain sanity and appear great at all times. It was simple always smile, be perfectly beautiful physically, answer the inevitable question of "how are you" with "everything is fine or great," never cry or appear sad, and stay extraordinarily busy, too busy to make friends, talk extensively or reveal only the surface of who I am. That would leave very little time for any true dialogue or questions about who I was or where I was from. It worked like a fine tuned instrument much of the time. When it would crack, only my closest family would know and I could always blame it on PMS, or exhaustion or any manner of simple common issues that could make one react out of sorts. I would quickly, push down those unwanted feelings and reminders by getting more and more involved in anything that did not have to shine a magnified light on me.

I am sure you would like me to get on with the story, but please be patient with me; yes, I am stalling because it is not easy to write the details of my life at forty-two years of age without careful preparation and recalling my friends who helped me survive in the moment. I will need them to get through this book.

What friends you ask? The ones that I created to help me survive, I learned to disappear or now formerly titled disassociate so that I would not become consumed by the trauma, it is a survival tactic, but when can I start living and stop surviving? I need them now because it is difficult to write of the horrors and know that you are the victim without escaping into one who can manage. The pain rolls through my body as a tornado does through a Midwest mobile home park; destroying every part of my crumbling shack called life. The tears become uncontrollable and the rain seems to have never known sunshine.

So why write it you may ask? I am writing it completely for selfish reasons, and totally without regard for another, not to ostracize myself although I am aware of the fact that it may, but from whom I am not sure because I am virtually already alone. I write my story not for pity or for others to judge my sanity, but so that I may utter the words that have been harbored for so long in the black box hidden deep in the heart of my engine. I want to scream, "I was raped, beaten, molested and sold" and not to feel that it was my fault or ashamed for being weak. I want to cry freely for the part of my life that was taken; I want to let the tears flow and not have to be strong. I have been enslaved by my own refusal to remember and now I desire to be free from fear and begin to live. I no longer choose to exist with smiles that mask my pain. I Alison Sloan want to be whole for me, not for others who require that I am compliant with their edicts and request. I want to laugh for the sake of funny. All of these are dreams, how can I scream, or cry for I must be strong and have very limited expressions of emotion for they continue to be signs of weakness and cost me opportunities that I have worked hard to obtain. I have to find a way take off the mask and allow feelings to flow naturally running may not work forever.

PART IV

RESEARCH ON CHILD ABUSE SUGGESTS THAT
RELIGIOUS BELIEFS CAN FOSTER,
ENCOURAGE, AND JUSTIFY THE ABUSE OF
CHILDREN. WHEN CONTEMPT FOR SEX
UNDERLIES TEACHINGS THAT INFLUENCE
FAITH, LOVE, AND TRUST IN OTHERS, A
BREEDING GROUND FOR ABUSE WITHOUT HOPE
IS CREATED.

CHAPTER 10

*Who watches out for little black girls
and boys? Where are their protectors? Who
owns their bodies, and when will they get to
be children and not property. Will they ever
hear My cries?*
PGHG

RAINN Analysis

The Rape, Abuse, and Incest National
Organization provides data on the number of
reported abuse victims that one out of every
six American women has been the victim of an
attempted or completed rape in her lifetime
(RAINN.org). This number sounds alarming;
however, I am pretty sure my name and the
names of my sisters are not a part of the
data. RAINN.org also suggests that only 18.8
percent of rapes that occur are to Black
women, with the largest group being white
women. However, I again suggest that
RAINN.org and most other organizations that
fight the battles to protect the virtue and
innocence of girls and women, do not have

the numbers correct for Black women. We are less likely to report our victimization for the real fear of reprisal including death, not from strangers but often from the men who made us; our fathers, or those who are a part of our bloodline; our uncles, brothers, cousins, and all the strangers that become part of our extended families. They extend themselves into our bedrooms, steal our innocence, and walk away without remorse. Was this a learned action by the slave masters who stole their women and dared them to say or do anything to protect the woman they purported to love? Now is it their turn to prove that they can bring internal scars that do not heal to their daughters, sisters, and the mothers of their children?

Report, report what? I remember only understanding what so many victims understand "if you ever tell anybody you will pay with your life." Fear of additional abuse was expected, but the fear for my own life had a paralyzing power over me that would not be easily diminished by the protective faces of the teachers who said, "You can talk to me, I won't let anything happen to you this is a safe place." In 1979, there was no safe place and in 2010, there is no safe place for a child to cry out for help, parents have the power to "rear their children as they choose." At forty years old those threats sound like just a part of the Black vernacular, but at four or five or even twelve, they sounded like law and with the beatings from my oppressors I felt like they were trying to leave me within inches of life so that I would know not to "try" them. Therefore, when I read about the reports from great agencies like RAINN.org I want them to know that they are missing a whole group of girls who are now women and suffer daily in our parenting, relationships, trust, families, work, and all other areas of life but our reports are not a part of their statistical data.

Black Girls

Research conducted by Gail Wyatt (1997) in "Stolen Women: Reclaiming Our Sexuality, Taking Back Our Lives", and Robin D. Stone (2005) who wrote "No Secrets No Lies: How Black Families Can Heal from Sexual Abuse", along with national statistics provides insight into the experiences of Black Survivors. Wyatt (1997) provided an insightful look into the history of African-Americans of victimization and sexual abuse dating back to their initial arrival in this country as slaves.

Gail Wyatt (1997) writes, "Black men were forced to have sex with random black women to reproduce like animals. This was done to produce more slaves to work the plantation. Slave masters did not care if these women were their mothers, daughters or sisters. Furthermore, it was not uncommon for the slave master to father his slave daughter's children". Additionally, she states that it was common for black men to form relationships with women from other plantations so that they did not have to witness their women being raped by the slave master (1997). Robin Stone (2005) adds that for survival our ancestors learned to act complacent and submissive, to put on a mask to navigate through life. To talk about sexual attacks could result in lashings, sale or even death. So not talking showed a bravado that was passed down from generation to generation. Today this is called splitting or disassociation (2005).

Both of these author's capture the historical foundation of sexual assault within the Black community. Yet, history is not easily forgotten and more often than not, it seems only become standard and acceptable practice. As portrayed in the movie version of "For Colored Girls Who Have Considered Suicide When The Rainbow is Enuf by Ntozake Shange (1989) and put on the big screen by Tyler Perry in 2010, black women and girls lives are never the same after sexual assault. Alison Sloan experiences these outcomes daily; the incidents that raped her of a childhood and stole her future are always attached to her like a coat of paint on a wall that can be covered but not removed.

Stone (2005) provides insight into the culture of abuse in the black family and the message that "*Children are expendable*". She states that it is common for their needs to be irrelevant and they are to be seen and not heard. They are told, to stay in a child's place, because this is grown folks business and children should be seen and not heard. The struggle of taking trying to maintain basic living needs invoke that message that children are not the priority until they become disconnected from expressing problems or feelings. Whether implied or verbalized, the parent conveys, "I have so much going on myself that I just can't handle any more problems. (2005)"

In addition to being, expendable children are often given the most isolating message that forms their life reactions. "Whatever goes on within these four walls remains within these four walls." A long history of others prying into the lives of Black families led to a lack of trust for authority. Authority in the form of slave masters, welfare workers, social workers, teachers, prosecutors, judges, police, parole officers, doctors and employers appeared to persecute, take, lie and kill Black families thus trust of any of these groups was and continues to be the greatest hindrance to reporting incidents of abuse.

Allie was told at the age of seven that she had to be made ready and if she told, she would be beaten. Stone (2005) expresses the impact of this message when she writes, "some survivors are told that they were being prepared for relationships with men" and that it was their job to prepare them for what was to come. Blacks were taught that with social service agencies prying into our homes, police, etc., many of us consider our homes off-limits. What goes on in the home, stays in the home? Therefore, the rule was to keep all who would challenge a parent's authority over their children out of their business.

Allies' first experience with sexual abuse was at the age of four. She was taught like many child victims that her body did not belong to her. "Go ahead give your uncle a kiss." The expectation was not to go against the parent's authority or risk getting a beating or worse for "disrespecting" an adult. Allie got the message that an adult's needs were far more important than her needs. Blacks have often lived in a communal setting with extended family and strangers like cousins, aunts, uncles, grandparents, etc., which, many times exposed the child to a potential predators. With hands tied to cultural values, holding us stronger than truth, afraid of airing what is considered by some our "dirty laundry" in public. This makes it easier to blame the victim or not believe the victim at all, in an attempt to protect the reputation of the race or suspected perpetrator.

Part V

THE INDULGENCES OF MARDI GRAS (FAT TUESDAY) ALLOWS FOR AN OPEN CELEBRATION WHERE ALL THINGS ARE ALLOWED PRIOR TO ASH WEDNESDAY, THE BEGINNING OF LENT OR FASTING. FOR ME INDULGENCE OF OTHERS TO MY BODY DID NOT END IN A DAY BUT AFTER FIFTEEN YEARS OF BEING SOLD WITH THE MASKS NEEDED TO SURVIVE OTHERS SEXUAL INDULGENCES. ENDING THE PHYSICAL ABUSE OPENED THE DOOR FOR TORTURE OF THE MIND, NOT FASTING FROM PAIN. WHEN WILL THE FAST BEGIN?

CHAPTER 11

*Everyone has multiple masks worn on the
occasion most suited; those whose
experiences harm the very core of who they
are wear multiple masks on each day and
often are unaware of the change.*
—PGHG

Allie struggled to share her
experiences; she chose to give space to
those who protected her from the reality of
what was happening. They remain within her
continue to protect her. Allie uses an
unfamiliar voice; because her voice was shut
down before she recognized its sound and has
only begun to surface as an audible sound
that has authority. Prior to now, those that
dwelt within separated and divided,
themselves into distinct persons who managed
her existence like a well-run business. She
named those who protected her and guided her
through the blind under growth that lurked
around every corner but seems to go

unnoticed by all except those who live in its filth.

I am not crazy, it is obvious to me that you must be thinking that I have schizophrenia, or multiple personality disorder, or any other label that we assign to the broken in our society who strive to find a way to cope when society forgets that we exist. I do want you to know that I understand your judgment. However, I do ask that you afford me the decency of reading my story in its entirety before you lower the gavel.

I believe nomenclature is very important in defining the character of a person. I was born as Alison Michelle Sloan; I understand that I was given the name at birth, but it was not added to my birth certificate until February 7, 1975, four years and nearly four months after I was born. I have asked why but no one seems to

have an answer. Alison means "Noble Kind",
it is the strongest part of me and has
helped me be resilient. It gave me the
strength to fight for safety. Michelle means
one "who is like God". The only thing I
understood about God was that he was
everywhere and would comfort me when no
comfort existed.

This is where the coping mechanisms
made life bearable and Laural helped me get
through the "preparation experience. She
came first to comfort me, and allow the
child in me exist in my mind. I did not have
the option to play or laugh but would hide
and cry holding my knees tightly to my chest
trying to muffle the sounds so no one would
hear my pain. I was found distressed and
laying in the fetal position dreaming of
hiding in the trees and hoping not to be
noticed. Gaddi is an immature adolescent
who is angry at life. Gaddi seems to feel

that she's never had the chance to live a normal teen life so her arrival is explosive, angry and irrational. Jerica is the strong, brash, no nonsense professional with a self-assured intellectual ability that captivates an audience in minutes and make a two-hour lecture feel like five minutes. Jerica is kind for the audience and her ability to hold it together is baffling. I am so glad that she is a part of me that she can take the role of holding it all together even when I feel helpless. Finally, the worst but most protective of all is Leila. Leila is the alter ego who protected me from many of the beatings that came with being enslaved. Leila could put on a malleable persona that made her appear weak and desirable without complaining. Her presence covers fear by emanating an exacerbated level of sexuality, eroticism, moderate self-confidence and superciliousness. Leila was sexy, beautiful and strong, she could do any job without feeling, she prevents me from remembering all of the abuse, and sometimes I wish she were not so protective.

Again I ask you not to prejudge the protective manifestations of my brokenness, for their actions were all about survival "by any means necessary" as stated by Malcolm X. When melded together not as a puzzle but as a perfect pearl unscarred, a holistic and existentialist view of who I am can be seen.

CHAPTER 12

"I believe in everything until it's disproved. So I believe in fairies, the myths, dragons. It all exists, even if it's in your mind. Who's to say that dreams and nightmares aren't as real as the here and now?"
— *John Lennon*

No information that is revealed in this recollection is to be considered absolute and without other views. However, it is critical to understand the unmitigated fact that it is my truth as I recall it. Truth is another one of those obscure words that can be disguised as fact. Yes, this is my truth. As you read, remember that fact and truth are both from my perspective and my memory. Indeed, there is proof, apologies from family perpetrators themselves who painstakingly express their reasons for committing the heinous acts along with my mother's acknowledgement and simultaneous deflection of blame. She answers the questions through the lenses of self-saving memories that exonerate her from any, and all responsibility. Proof is as important to me as it is for you, obtaining confirmation was critical. My box was partitioned and closed for many long years, neither Laurel, Gaddi, Jerica, Leila nor was Alison aware of the others making it difficult to bring them together. The competition for attention makes Allie appear to be erratic when triggers from any of the experiences surface causing my protectors to vie for the protective position. With only partial memories I could only apologize in a self-effacing way that would make it my fault, not that of another. I do not want to bring pain to others; therefore, the demons that haunt my nights and lead to reactions that I cannot explain only beg forgiveness.

My life was a mirage that placed necessity in front of thinking and feeling.

As a wife, mother and student there was
limited time to think about the past. The
moments when it emerged were many more than
I realized often in the midst of life's
normal transitions. Many I was prepared for
but not all of the preparation in the world
prepared me for the impact of my children
leaving home. My older daughter Mia was in
her senior year of high school. She was
mine and she was never to leave me. As
irrational, as this sounds no part of Alison
Sloan could understand what was happening.
Yes, college was always in the plan, the
plan just did not include me being stripped
of my Love Child. Adding misery to the
situation my baby girl, my funny genius
Bella, had been accepted into one of the
most prestigious residential high schools in
the country and was also leaving. It was
too much, who needed me, and what would I do
that mattered? Yes, I loved education but

the same year I was completed my Ph.D. and with nothing and no one, I crashed. David could not understand the drastic changes that had been growing worse over the past couple of years, we argued more than ever and I was so cruel to him. He is so strong but he was being crushed by my out of control behavior. I believed I had nothing and my best efforts had failed; I wanted to die.

The nightmares were overwhelming and now my days were filled with terror. I could no longer push the truth out of my head the flood of memories crashed through my subconscious and were in the center of my conscious world. Feeling completely out of control, I fell into the grip of depression, self-loathing and hopelessness. Gaddi arrived and took me to the one place where I was in control. Refusing food made me strong, and the purging of any that was forced gave me power over my world. I did not notice the extreme weight loss and focused on exercising my body until I felt nothing. Laural has always helped to to run away from the pain into our secret place in the trees. Alone I had no one but my protectors, Jerica went to work every day and Leila made sure that I felt the touch of another. It was all surreal Alison was safe and walked through the mirage unaware of the activities of the others. I maintained a high actively engaged lifestyle, which included three to five hours of exercise daily. Running through trails where no one could find me was my great escape and I would run until pain or exhaustion overtook me. When the weather would not allow an outdoor venture I would exercise for hours lifting weight that was too heavy, running on the treadmill for an hour and followed by an hour of elliptical and another thirty minutes of the stair climber, all just not to feel. I succumbed to their control. I gave in to the pain that I had avoided so long, but nothing I did seem to shut the memories down. Emaciated and broken I could not understand why David loved me even after I moved out, he would not let a day pass without calling, visiting or just checking in. I did not understand and do not now, why would someone care so much for trash like me, what was their plan? My children and extended family believed that I would be dead in months I desired nothing less. I was completely emaciated with sunken cheeks and bones revealed where flesh once made them unnoticeable. No one including myself understood what was happening, I was out of control, and death was not my savior Jesus Christ the Son of God's plan and he would not let me die. My husband, children, and family fought harder for my life than I did, for all I could do was walk in a zombie like state while life happened and every evening I read the Book of Philippian's. I have no rational reason why, but I prayed a lot to feel something other than pain and to understand why I was on this earth. I do not know the answers but Paul's words brought me comfort and over time strengthen me. Each day I worked, cried, prayed, read Philippians repeatedly until, I found the strength to try.

I returned home with David who although struggling to understand what was happening, he embraced me and welcomed me home. After returning home, I sought help from my primary doctor who was afraid for my life, he referred me to the Eating Disorder outpatient clinic, to a nutritionist, therapist, psychiatrist, and placed under his care. I went to the eating disorder clinic, but was not ready to talk or give up my control. I was constantly given reasons to be self-assured, given nutritional advice and weighed. I was angry if I gained and they were happy. Weekly, I was to log my physical activity level and document my eating and daily feelings. This was too much and after six-weeks, I stopped going. I understood perfectly everything they said, I am an avid reader and researcher. Therefore, I knew how many calories to eat to gain or lose weight and what a nutritional meal consisted of the hard part was hearing week after week that I was not doing enough to improve my health. This bothered me because my blood work showed no signs of problems, blood pressure was normal and my heart rate was fine, therefore what did they want from me. My feelings did not matter so I simply felt forced to go hear all of the things I needed to work on, and they were in charge. I do not like to lose control over my life,

not now, not at 40 no damn way was someone
going to force me to do anything. I was
tired of driving 50 miles one-way each week
to hear that I needed to eat and gain
weight. They constantly told me the
outcomes of my behavior as if I did not
know. My death sentence was that my internal
organs mostly my heart was being harmed all
was well, they saw the paperwork. I quit,
just stopped going, I was tired of someone
telling me what to do with me. Eventually, I
was encouraged by my therapists to talk to a
psychiatrist to help me "manage the
depression and minimize the nightmares",
prescribed Prozac and Klonopin I began to
stop feeling and just existing.

CHAPTER 13

No trace of slavery ought to mix with the studies of the freeborn man. No study, pursued under compulsion, remains rooted in the memory.
- Plato

The impacts of the events of my life are many and one of the most horrible effects is memory. I heard many times "Alison, hey Alison" only to turn and have someone coming toward me with a face that reflects joy and surprise at seeing me. The closer they become the more nervous I am because I do not understand why this stranger knows my name. "You don't remember me do you?" Is always the question when they are close, before I respond I hear that we attended school together, we were in the same courses, we were best friends, and all I see is a face that brings me fear because I have no memory from their descriptions or their face? I hear myself asking them what kind of person I was and what they know about me, it makes me feel weird and I believe they feel that something is wrong with me; maybe I am crazy. On several occasions, the person has tried to force me to remember and I completely lost it, I was afraid and left the event crying because I could not and cannot remember. Therefore, my truth is undeniable because the very nature of a memory is that which is recalled from the long/short term internal vision of the one sharing the information. I am not saying that my truth is absolute just that it was not merely my memory but also in depth research and contact with primary sources who were involved. It is certain that I have included memories that continue to emerge from the box as I reconcile the information and try to put the pieces together to become whole. There is no need for embellishment, the fact is the magnitude of these truths are so overwhelming that writing this causes my heart to pound and my body to feel mechanical; these words are not free flowing they are painstakingly terrifying because of the vivid imagery they bring to my cognition.

Just as Kasi Lemmons (1997) used tapestry as a metaphor for memory at the end of Eve's Bayou: "The truth changes color depending on the light and tomorrow can be clearer than yesterday. Memory is a selection of images, some elusive, others printed indelibly on the brain. Each image is like a thread, each thread woven together to make a tapestry of intricate texture and the tapestry tells a story and the story is our past." My authenticity is now a "tapestry" with beauty, pain, and ugly that makes the total of my past. A past filled with the look of a coastal sky just as a hurricane approach when the sun, dark

clouds, and white fluffy clouds all compete
for the sky. Unaware that there is a
hurricane moving in to override and destroy
each of them, and once it has been satisfied
it leaves with the understanding that the
sun will come back to brighten the ocean sky
for another day.

Part VI

THERE CAN BE NO BETTER MEASURE OF OUR
INTEGRITY THAN THE WAY WE PROTECT,
LOVE, TEACH AND HONOR OUR CHILDREN, AND
NO GREATER FAILING ON OUR PART THAN TO
ALLOW THEM TO BE SUBJECTED TO VIOLENCE,
ABUSE OR EXPLOITATION.

CHAPTER 13

*"Child abuse casts a shadow the length
of a lifetime."*
- Herbert Ward

Bringing you into my life is hard, thus
you may find the change of tone or voice as
I put it into words. God has so graciously
provided me with avenues to survive and
writing is reliving and too often re-
experiencing what my brain could not
withstand. The trauma that made up the
first twenty years of my life is livable
because he helped to take the pain, even if
it involved separating me into pieces. I was
allowed the opportunity to become a forced
participant and a pain free observer
throughout my childhood and teen years
through these protective character traits. I
am no angel as you will see but at forty-two
years of age, I am finally safe, not fully
free but surely safe.

I met Laural, Gaddi, Jerica and Leila at different times in life and all were supportive in the way that I needed at the time. The first time I met Laural was that awful summer day in the woods when I was 6 years old, my two older brothers lured me into the woods in the back of our home with promises of a secret only for me. My excitement and my age did not give me pause to imagine anything would take place, but I would see a surprise; maybe I would see a playhouse that they had built, or a new stream to swing across or better a big tree that I could climb, but I never felt fearful. I do not remember everything, for I left my body and the pain on the ground and hid in the trees. I was not emotionally present, and escaping the moment by sitting in a tree made the rape not imaginary. I was watching as they took turns penetrating my seven-year-old virgin body, but then Laural rescued me and I sat quietly in the tree. With her, all feeling stopped efforts to cry out for help ended, tears dried, and I sat on the great tree branch and watched. I watched, as one brother held me down while the other brother delightfully entered my body. I do not know how long or when my mind and body reconnected, but when they did I was in the leaves, in pain and naked. That was the day Laural became my best friend.

Leila is different she made life not exist. She is very warm and sexy, she is beautiful and has a sway when she walks that no one can ignore. Leila knows that she is desired and does not tease but pleases. I met her at the toughest time of my life. Without her existence I would have died. She always took over when I first entered the house where all the girls were. When beatings were for general practice, and strange people would be on me when my screams yielded more cruelty than bearable, Leila just took it all away. The scars from the lash remained but I could only see them, I was numb and could not remember what happened but I saw others with similar scars that they received when they did not do or say something right. So, I must have been non-compliant, but today as I write I only remember the beginning and the end and I cry. Leila trained me to stop fighting the inevitable because it would only bring additional pain and possibly death. She was there for all of the punches and took me away while she endured the person on top of me, kicking me, or touching my young body that was not developed but eagerly desired. Leila is provocative and beautiful she would show no signs of fear she would become completely sweet and intoxicatingly vivacious. Leila knew how to avoid beatings, punches, and starvation; she knew how to be compliant, seductive and desired. Nothing could completely prevent me from being hit or sodomized some people were just evil, but Leila taught me not feel just be. It was not a way out of being photographed, exploited or raped, but it was a way to minimize the bruises. Leila took a long time to arrive because I believed I could fight back and always run away.

Gaddi is a spirited, often called hardheaded girl with an attitude that will catch up with her. If Gaddi could get away from something unpleasant, all she needed was a brown paper bag filled with what she believed was important. As Gaddi, states' running away was just life; it was what I was supposed to do when the pain was too much and I could map my escape. I would focus on the when and how to get away for weeks, but I have yet to think about the where. I do not ever remember being asked if

I wanted to go somewhere or live with anyone and actually felt that, my answer actually had a chance of being heard. If the question was posed at all it was in a tone that did not need an answer "you want to go stay with....right?" I never went anywhere but one place "home" it took me years to realize that I was not welcomed there, for within months of running home I was in someone else's clutches with guardianship papers, a birth-certificate and a single instruction "you better be a good girl and do what you are told" yes sir/ma`am. The first time I began successfully running away in third grade when I was about eight years old. She would always explain that she did not like the place we were, I think bad things were happening and she wanted out not like what my brothers' did but my work. I remember this as I write, which is somewhat scary. I remember having to wash baseboards until they were "virgin" bridal white, raking leaves until not one remained on the two acres of forested land, sleeping in a locked attic and enough food to live. Beatings were relentless and the switches on my bare body left horrible whelps, but that was okay, until I was promised a beating for going on a forbidden school trip that was paid for by the school. I was in trouble for "making the school think that I needed their help", I could not take another whooping, I was just scared and hopeless, I just wanted to die, Gaddi arrived.

Seeking refuge at home always seemed possible, yet, within the year, I had a new address where love for me did not reside only expectations. I was never allowed to remain at home with my siblings and parents; I do not know why and might never actually know. I do not know how I was sent from place to place, but I am sure there was a financial transaction because each month there was a visit from my father. He never got out of the car but the person would always go to the car and after a brief conversation and a "handshake", he would wave from the window and leave.

Enslaved by the constant knowledge of being alone the only choice to me was to pray for mercy that I might maintain a piece of mind. A simple request that was forever elusive. I became very anxious and nervous, striving to be the perfect student with the hope that "A's" would mask my truth. In one quick breath I would be called intelligent, and in the next arrogant and both had merit. Intelligence was easy, being smart was as simple as following instructions, and I was an expert. Arrogance, not so easy, it is difficult to maintain a strong barrier for protection, when the desire is for a hug. But mostly I lived in terror knowing that regardless of my embellishments I knew what would happen and I could not cover the scars that ravaged my mind and my soul, therefore I placed them neatly in the box and buried it deep in my heart. Yes, I understand the irony of putting fake and normal together, but how else would I survive school.

Each had a time and a circumstance that brought them to the forefront. Judge me if you like, but not until you have had twenty years of abuse; then after your judgment pray for my peace. I understand that mercy was always there because I am here today, but during that time my eyes, my back, my legs, my face and my mind did not know it existed. The boots that made contact with my ribs, and the fists that met my cheeks, and the extension cord that planted rows on my back disguised Mercy and yet I cried for it as the wrath of many tore at my body.

It was not only the tenants at the new addresses that had expectations, but I too always anticipated that things would somehow be different in this space. I am not a slow learner academically, but in life, I was always the optimist. I always looked and believed the best would come out of people and they would be kind and caring if I was "good", they would not hurt me if I listened and tried really hard, I always thought that I could be a good girl and they would not hurt me if I was nice. I tried really hard not to make people mad and I was nice I did good work and did not talk back or do what I was not told to do, but it did not matter, and it does not pay to be good, you still get hurt. Gaddi is ready to flee if danger is coming but she always thought that the next place would be better and went into the door with her eyes closed and her heart ready to be received. Innocence and optimism ruled, you might call it ignorance, yet I believed and that allowed me to push past quit. Those days and nights where the best that happened was that I was hungry or cold, always deceived me into believing that the next day would be better if I just tried harder. On those nights when all was wrong, my prayers were much different, on those nights, I felt hopeless and regardless of the personality that emerged, I could not be comforted, I prayed for death to overtake me and let me be at peace, but death would not honor my plea.

Part VII

UNWANTED CHILDREN HAVE A HARD TIME FROM THEIR INCEPTION, THEY ARE IRREPARABLY DAMAGED PSYCHOLOGICALLY, EMOTIONALLY STUNTED AND OFTEN PHYSICALLY ABUSED BY PARENTS AND EXTENDED FAMILY MEMBERS THAT CLEARLY, DO NOT WANT THEM, BUT "RAISED" THEM BECAUSE OF OBLIGATION, NOT LOVE.

CHAPTER 14

*Home is where our memories are cemented and
our expectations grow wings; an ever
changing home interrupts our reliance on its
stability and our safety.*
—PGHG

On Sunday, October 18 in the year of
1970, just before noon 11:40 a.m., according
to the record of my birth, I arrived. My
father was forty-four and my mother was
twenty-nine. Because my birth record is
incomplete and I could not remember where I
lived, I conducted personal research to
confirm my locations. I requested my
medical records and academic records. This
was an arduous task since I lived in three
states and documentation was replete with
gaps, including huge blocks where there are
no school records. I must state the obvious,
I was not born in a century or decade where
documentation was nonexistent, in the 1970's

and 80s records of birth and education were required. My brother who is eleven months older and the one who is 17 months younger have complete histories. Therefore, it is normal for me to be confused because my historical records are subpar. However, because of my research my earliest record of my existence was a shot record where I received my first shots signed by my mother. I cannot explain the birth certificate, but eventually, sometime in 1975, my name was added to my birth record, and I must presume that it was because I was preparing to attend school. I have also learned that the hospital noted on my birth certificate is incorrect and I was not born at home. With a birth certificate that states "information taken from previous record" and without being reviewed or signed by a parent, I must be an enigma.

Per information gathered from relatives including my mother I was brought home to the little farm house that we lived in as sharecroppers in a very small rural southern community where tobacco was the cash crop. It remains a small rural town where cattle dot the sides of the road and tobacco continues to be a significant agricultural crop. I remember going to the tobacco field and picking up leaves in the barn and pulling tobacco off stalks that had large green worms on them. I enjoyed all living creatures and played with the worms when I should have been picking up leaves that fell when the tobacco was hung. I was not old enough to be in the field at that house, but by the age of three or four, everyone was expected to work some aspect of the crops. Not one of these crops did we own as sharecroppers, it seemed that we worked for someone different every year. I am grateful not to be in anyone's tobacco field or have to smell the scent of cow manure in the early summer.

My earliest memories have no real timeline just a hodgepodge of actions that seem to flit in and out of my memory as I hear stories from family or drive through the country part of the rural towns we lived in, or view family albums. I remembered nothing about my life prior to six or seven years of age until I was in a therapy session where a very familiar story changed while I was in an EMDR state. The opening story of my uncle who lived with us was never scary, but just did not make sense until I mentally relived the horror. Blocking out some memories were good for me, when they returned it was as if I was the little girl that cried out in pain in the chicken house and got in trouble.

My mother proudly exclaims that I was a "beautiful baby with a head full of black curls" she says that I was often with a family named Charles and Mary Hinson that worked with them in the fields and worshipped with my parents at church because they thought I was so "precious". I am told that the Hinson's loved me so much that I spent many weekends with them and their daughters. They would take me to their church when they did not attend my parents' church New Jerusalem and would dress me in beautiful dresses just like their daughters, "they really loved you". My mother said that they loved me so dearly and would "dress me like their girls" because I "fit" right into their family. Long thick curly hair and cocoa complexion, and a short round body, she said, "no one would know that you were not their child."

I find great pleasure in knowing that for my first few years of life I enjoyed some pleasure, it was irrelevant who provided it but the fact that it existed is nice. If I was loved as a child, I do not remember but I do remember never being at home. It is very sad to think about it now because if it is true that was probably the most joy I had as a child, and yet I have no memory of it and no pictures to verify the information. Only the words of family confirm the information.

At two years of age, we moved to a different sharecropper's house that my mother call Mr. Johnson. I have no memories of this house, it is said that we lived there a year before we moved to house near the interstate, in 1974. I do remember this house for one reason only, I must have been three or maybe four, but I remember the house was another slab wood house, similar to all of the houses we lived in, it had outdoor plumbing and we slept on the floor. What makes this house memorable are two things: the long dirt road that we treaded daily to get to the fields and the huge oak tree that stood in the yard and provided shade for the whole house. I remember one day just standing in the front yard being enamored by that tree. I stood there in my cut off shorts and dusty shirt with two big ponytails in my hair, pointing in awe at what seemed to me to be the coolest worm ever. It was huge, long, and black almost shiny it was beautiful. It eased around the branches and had part of its body around a branch and its head hanging off the tree just looking at me. I stood there oblivious to anyone else and the wonder of that creature was fascinating. I faintly remember hearing my brothers' screaming and seeing my father running toward the tree, he pushed me back from the tree and in a dazed state a loud popping sound like firecrackers rang loudly in my ear and I saw the beautiful worm fall from the tree. Still in a stupor sitting on the ground where I was pushed, I received a terse lesson on what a snake was and how "they were nothing to play with". Little did I know how that lesson that would have more meaning in my life than any other would. "A snake is not a worm, you cannot play with them, some of them are poisonous and all of them can wrap around your body and cut off your breath and kill you".

The next year we moved again it was 1975 and we moved to sharecrop the land of a man I remember as Mr. Simpson. I can only say that at five years old I learned a life lesson that seemed to cement my future. It was not in Sadler Elementary where I attended kindergarten it was at home. The house on Mr. Simpson's property was a bigger than the others; of course, there were more of us at the time, thirteen to be exact. My parents' also seemed to always have family members who needed a place to "stay for a while" usually uncles that were related to my mother and some that I do not know how they were related, but we all were there. There were four more children younger than I was at the time and total there were ten children and one on the way. Each night we were locked upstairs in a one-window room where there were mattresses on the floor and buckets to use the bathroom. There were three girls and five boys who slept on used flat mattresses while the adults and two infant boys remained downstairs.

I have already established the fact that I was a precocious and inquisitive child who did not manage boredom well. Therefore, how do you run or explore locked in a small room with seven other people who were sleeping, when you have already slept enough. I could not go downstairs that was not an option, because the door was locked from the outside. I would have climbed out of the window, but if I hurt myself, or made noise, or were caught out of the room I would surely get a whooping. So what is a five-year-old to do? Well this five-year-old had secured a secret tool to be used in a time of need, and this was a time of need.

With a hint of moonlight sneaking through the closed curtain of the very dark space, there was just enough light to brighten an otherwise dark room enough for me to find "something to do." In the dark hours just before the sun would rise from the East over the horizon and encapsulate the entire room with its beams of wonder, I realized there was a small even tiny slither of cotton sticking out of the mattress I had slept on. If I had something else to do this

would not have bothered me but I did not and
therefore I had to fix the bed. I was, and
continue to be a bit obsessive compulsive
and unfilled time was not good for me.
Therefore, I determined that the cotton had
to go. I tried to remove it by pulling it
off, but the more I pulled at the cotton the
more came out of the bed. I no longer had a
little piece of cotton hanging out of my
mattress but a huge piece (in reality as I
reflect it probably was not huge). Seeing
what I had done assured me that I would be
finding a switch as soon as someone saw it,
but my "genius mind" said that would not be
happening! I would make sure that no one
ever saw the mess that I had made trying to
get that piece of cotton off my bed. I took
out my secret weapon and pondered as best as
a five-year-old could . . . whooping or get
rid of the cotton; which would you choose?
I chose to get rid of the cotton. Sitting

there with my nightclothes on, a tee shirt and panties, I knew that I had to hurry up before the suns beams overtook the moons rays. My secret weapon had been hidden for a while because it was *my secret* and no one else's. I gingerly lifted the edge of the mattress very quietly as not to make noise that would awaken anyone else. I took out the book of matches that I had secured from somewhere, just because I loved the scent of the match when it struck the black line on the top of the little book that held the matches. I figured that one day when I was alone I would just strike them all one after the other to smell the wonderful scent that emerged from the touch of the phosphorous coated match tip to the "red phosphorous" strip on the match book. But, now I had an emergency that needed to be taken care of to avoid the pain of a dogwood switch cutting across my short legs and back. Quietly, and with precision I struck the match and carefully inhaled the smell as I held the end of the cotton that was farther from the mattress and lit the part closest so that it could burn the cotton but not the bed.

I was rational and intentional as any scientist at my age. When the fire and its beautiful hues of orange and blue and shades of red touched the cotton everything went wrong. The fire went both ways on the cotton, it burned my hand because I did not let go of the match fast enough, and my effort to put the fire out with the bed cover was futile. It seemed to get bigger and bigger and bigger, I tried to put it out quietly but it kept growing and it was on the bed and I was being burnt because I kept trying to put it out with my cover and it did not work, I was definitely getting a whooping.

Eventually, the others woke and started to scream, they did not try to help me put it out they just pulled me off the bed and everyone ran to the bottom of the steps to the locked door. The fire seemed to get bigger because even at the door, we could not breathe and it was all smoky, we could see the reddish orange flames above us but we were stuck at the door unable to escape. The fire spread swiftly to the other mattresses and the upstairs became a thick fog of smoke. My siblings and I screamed, cried, and banged on the door, but it seemed like an eternity before it was finally opened and we were free from the fog that was now burning the walls, floor, and ceiling of the house. Without hesitation, everyone pointed at me (no honor among siblings) and although I had burns, I was getting ready to have whelps. On that day, I deserved a beating but when the doctor asked my father if he gave me a whooping, I realized that doctors were not my friend. I sat in the hospital looking down thinking "what kind of doctor asks if a child got a whooping?" This lesson solidified my lack of trust in authority figures and I learned always to do what they said because they are not my friends.

Of course, we had to move again and because this was the summer after I finished kindergarten, it was okay because I was going to a new school. We moved to Mr. Murphy's property and the house was not quite as big but I liked it better because the house did not have but one floor and we could not be locked away. In 1976 and 77 we lived and sharecropped his land. We lived near my father's best friend Mr. Brown. He seemed nice; I do not remember much during my first-grade year at Lincoln Elementary but the fact that babies kept coming every year. By now there are almost seventeen kids living in one house. Nevertheless, it did not affect me much because most weekends and much of the summer I was at the home of the Hinson's

In December of 1977, we moved to the town of Mullins, it was in the same county but on the west side of the county. We moved to a house on Bambridge Road. It was a long dirt road where the 2.5 acres we moved onto had a small house and lots of trees. At the end of the dirt road flowed a large river, which led to many streams deep in the woods behind our house. When possible we would sneak away from the house far enough to avoid unnecessary work like cleaning up the yard. I was seven when we moved to Mullins, this house was not a sharecropper's home, my father actually purchased this land and home so that we would not have to move again according to my mother. I attended second grade at Mullins Primary school.

Part VIII

You think about child abuse and you think of a father viciously attacking a daughter or a son, but in my family it was my mother and my father. My mother, I would say, was a very absent non-caring, selfish person who has not changed. However my father was a ...very brutal abuser and disciplinarian.

CHAPTER 15

When one has not had a good father, one must create one.
—Friedrich Nietzsche

My Father's Family

I did not have the luxury of meeting my
paternal grandmother who died two days after
my birth from what appears to be diabetes,
or some other lifestyle illness. Now her
story is quite interesting. From the stories
shared with me by my aunts, mother, and
other close relatives; Grandmother Hattie
was no one to play with. She was quite tall,
very dark, very strict, and ran everything
like she was a military lieutenant. From my
father I am to understand that she was the
reason he ran away at such a young age and
refused to return until he was forced after
returning from WWII, and was a grown man of
twenty years old. I have often heard that I
look like my paternal Grandmother with a

different complexion, but I have the spirit of my grandfather, her husband. The combination only seemed to bring pain, because I was too afraid to stand up for myself and my close appearance to my grandmother seemed to make my father hate me.

I must have been two or three because I vaguely remember my paternal grandfather, who died in 1973, but he was really kind and I knew him as the peanut man. We would go to his house and he had a cow pasture that ran alongside his property and my brothers' and I loved to taunt the bull and we wanted to see if the bull would come charging us if we had on red or shook a red handkerchief at it. It never did, but we enjoyed trying. My grandfather would sit on the porch at his home and often at ours with jean overalls on and white curly hair. He was very fair some say he was a white man, but I do not know for sure. He was not as tall as my father and that may have been due to age or just genetics. He walked with a kind of bent over rounded shoulder stance and I do not remember him saying very many words. What I do remember about the only grandparent that I recall is that he would let me sit on his lap and while holding me his feeble hands had so many wrinkles that I felt like I tracing a map trying to find where they led. I never remembered him being angry, or even sad; he was just a really nice old man that gave us peanuts and showed an ounce of love to a crew of unloved children; unlike my father who always seemed angry and I never remember kindness or gentleness that was not followed or preceded by misery.

In October of 1981, there was this strange atmosphere at home, I had just returned but it was so thick with trouble that I did not dare ask what was happening.

I remember my father looking nothing like he did when he dropped me at his cousin's house a year earlier. He looked frail, sick, gaunt and even emaciated. At that time children were seen and not heard and I followed the rules accordingly. My father lived at this time in my older sister's trailer where a hospital bed had been placed rather than her normal furniture. I turned eleven on the eighteenth of October and the day was nothing special or worth remembering. However, what was worth remembering was the fact that we had two Thanksgivings and two Christmases, I did not understand, but I did not complain. Think about it all the food you want; sweet potato pie, macaroni and cheese, turkey, potato salad, so many cakes and deserts one would be crazy to not feel that we had died and gone to heaven.

That Christmas we received more than fruit bags with nuts, apples and oranges, we actually received gifts. I mean the best gifts in the world. We all got Big Wheels, mine was the Red Barron and it was different from everybody's except my brother who was only eleven months older than I and had just celebrated his twelfth birthday on the twenty-first of November. He got the Green Machine. It was the best, we did not think about food, or sickness or trouble or anything; including the ambulances that continued to come to our house and take my father away for weeks at a time. No we did not get it, in January they came more frequently and so did other relatives and they all went to see him in the trailer; no one came to see my mother in the house; just my father. She went with him to the hospital because it was required and the last time he came home he asked to talk to me after I had been in a fight with my oldest full sister.

I walked to the trailer with the fear of death following me, I did not know what my fate would be, and I thought I was getting in trouble. I walked in dusty as most of us were from playing outside and was sent into the bedroom where the hospital bed sat on the right side of the wall upon entering the room. Shiny metal rails, white bed covers and a shell of a man that stood 6'5" looking a pithy size of his former self. I stood just above the height of the bed and said "yes sir" and he told me to come closer and with fear I inched forward. His speech was low and I could barely understand his words, "Do you want to go stay with your Aunt in Florida?" The question was posed in such a nonchalant way as if I knew who my Aunt was or what Florida was, or as if I had a real choice in the decision. I said, "yes sir" and before the sun went down on January 25, 1982 I was with my Aunt preparing to go to this Florida place the next morning. I kissed him on the cheek; I do not know what made me do that but I did then and at his funeral a week later. He cringed in pain and stated, "don't be so rough" with a slight sideways smile I was dismissed from the room.

I ran back to my sisters' and told them the news as if I was the anchor from CNN, except I did not know the background of what any of it meant. I did not understand that he was dying and moments later, my sister ran back with the same news. Therefore, we left January 26, 1982 and returned on February 4, 1982 when he died of lung cancer.

I learned when I was much older the difficulty my mother experienced as a forty-year-old widow with fourteen children and five grandchildren that she was a wreck. My mother knew nothing about the bills associated with our home or the vehicles or the land. She did not know how to provide for her children or how to help herself. I promised myself then, and every day since then, that I would not be that person, the one that only functions on the wings of a stronger, bigger, and more controlling creature. In addition to the problems resulting from her limited knowledge of the families business affairs, my mother faced the wrath of my father's siblings.

My father's siblings made the wound only more infectious with their aggressive views about how the services should be managed, where, and by whom. Yes, my father and mother had all of the information prepared; however, my mother's weak spirit just gave in and allowed his sisters to decide everything about the funeral arrangements. Per my mother and older siblings, it was their intention to take the property and anything they believed belonged to my father. However, the strength of my oldest sister became evident and where my mother's weakness left gaping holes, she found her "Wonder Woman" bracelet and swore she would harm anyone who came and tried to take anything from our home.

My sister was and always had to be strong and resilient, but never had the opportunity to be a child after my mother chose my father. I thought for many years as a child that she was a "grown up" and was as terrified to get into mischief with her as I was with my father. However, when I grew into a young teenager, she was and has been my best friend, confidant, godmother to my children and sister unlike any other; she is my hero. Her strength and resolve has amazed me and guided me when no one else was there. After my father's death, my mother's depression worsened, and although the help that is available now for depression is prevalent, it was not so then. Therefore, within months all of her children were either in group homes, living with others through guardianship, or enrolled in job corp., military, or on the street.

I was in a fog about all of it, I had just returned home from a place I was not quite familiar with, and reflected on the multiple celebrations, which were very exciting. We had plenty of food and gifts, and less adult supervision; they always seemed to be going to the hospital. I do not know if any of the children knew what the hospital was but, the sirens that would come to our house and pick up my mother and father became common place. Till this very day with understanding of the emergency that the siren means I say a prayer for the family that had to call in an ambulance. I hate and love them, to me they mean death or life and for me they eventually meant death for my father, so the very sound makes me pray for the one they are helping.

I was sent to a strange home in a stranger city and returned a week later to attend what was called a funeral. I had never been to a funeral and seeing my father lying there, eyes closed, something said kiss his cheek, you will not hurt him this time; and I did. No tears, no recognition of family, I was alone in my own head again walking in a zombie like state being guided by a force outside of or inside me that made everyone else nonexistent. Just my father's cold face lying in a silver looking box with his legs covered by half of it and his arms tightly at his side, I was compelled to kiss his cheek and whisper "I love you." Again I walked back to my seat aware of the many people present but neither seeing nor hearing anything. I was in a stupor that made the entire event surreal.

Just as quickly as we arrived, we prepared to leave. I was not allowed to sit with my mother or visit afterwards; we went to my fathers' other sisters' home and after a few fitful hours of trying to sleep, my sister and I were on our way back to Florida. Now I had no grandparents, no father, and no mother to explain what happened or to just hold me when I was afraid. I did not understand why I could not go back to my mother.

CHAPTER 16

No mother would ever willingly sacrifice her sons for territorial gain, for economic advantage, for ideology.
—Ronald Reagan

But maybe her daughters for one tall handsome man.
—PGHG

Fond Memories of my Mother

I had fun during those visits with my granddad; and there was one other place where we could count on being children and having a blast; that was at my mother's aunt's home in a really small town in central Virginia. Aunt Blanch was the half sister of my grandmother Tayinita; who lived in an old house in a very rural small town of central Virginia. When we arrived at her small house it was fun all day, not your typical basketball, or stick ball fun but more like country fun. We would chase chickens with the goal of having it for dinner. We would explore the surrounding countryside and just run around and play as if being happy and laughing hard was our only purpose in life. Aunt Blanch was my maternal grandmother's sister.

I do not remember my maternal grandmother, although she died after I was born, but her death was tragic and leaves my mother empty when talking about it. Grandmother Tayinita also died in 1973 like my grandpa Jim. Unfortunately, her death was not of natural causes, per my mother, she died Christmas Eve, when she mistakenly used gasoline to light a kerosene heater, her long silky Cherokee hair that hung below her waist caught fire, and no one was around to save her.

I never met my maternal grandfather who died in 1962 presumably of a stroke or massive heart attack in the tobacco field. My maternal grandfather and grandmother were both alcoholics and at the time of his death, they had relocated from Virginia to Florida. My grandfather was a fair-skinned man who like many mulatto types and coloreds at the time worked on sharecropping farms and often moved annually. The house and fields have grown up where my maternal grandparents lived but the area is largely unused.

My mother lived with her mother until she met my father who was fifteen years her senior but she had already bore three children and was with child when they met. She stated that she went with him because he would take her and her four children. They were married when she was 25 and he was 40, however, they were remarried due to documentation that questioned the legality of the marriage nearly 10 years later.

Heritage versus Legacy

It is important to note that one's legacy is not defined by their heritage; but

I dare say that one's heritage defines their legacy. Heritage from its derivation denotes that it is literally something inherited with age, which begins at birth. Similarly, legacy is a word derived from the word legal and thus is not guaranteed or likely without the proper birthright. My heritage is rich and full of a multiplicity of mystery, crime, abuse and a wealth of confused love. My legacy is my own to claim, I cannot modify my heritage and I would not choose to. My experiences must not be hidden for to disown any part of me is to do a disservice to my children. With a heritage of pride and a legacy not to be forgotten it is critical that it be shared with future generations. I chose to live with fervor for my husband and my children sacrificing all to ensure their legacy would have value.

Now, I choose to live for Allie; the throw away, forgotten, raped of her innocence, her soul, her sweet laughter and her enduring beauty that if only God appreciates it will never be forgotten or taken away forcefully again. I will laugh with my husband and children; I will enjoy participating in and observing the changes that come into our life. I will laugh and learn how to feel tenderness, and expect respect, because I exist as a human member of a society that owes respect to everyone and it is especially kind to give it to its throwaways.

What about Me!

I never expected to bring calamity but it appears that I have done just that but I am "narcissistic". For adults like me home is hard to define home, but for children as I was it is worse. I constantly get the question "where are you from" and I have no idea how to answer the question without thinking of having no home. I continue to struggle with how to answer the question and prefer not to address the question, which brings its own questions. Not having a mother that comes to parent days or a father to make sure you will not be hungry, and the house you live in is not home it is merely a "wait" station that the time will run out on soon. I made a home with my husband and children, unsure of what to do as a mother, wife, or without chains of bondage I prayed much and hoped that I would not ruin the three people in my life who were giving me a chance. I am blessed to hear often that I am a great mother and a great wife, not only from those on the outside looking in but from those who are directly impacted by my actions.

It is very great that I hear these wonderful statements, but they are much clouded with statements that seem to be truer. I need validation and so I brag, I do not listen to anyone else because it is all about me, I live to be in others business. I am arrogant and thoughtless; I live in the past and ruin others' lives rather than getting over this and letting everyone else live their lives in peace. I apparently have convinced others' in the family that they have also been abused, without ever knowing that I had an influence on their lives. I struggle with these concepts because my intended aim is always, yes always to help. I did not think I needed validation because I boasted on my children. Arrogance always comes when Jerica is in the lead role. The mask is necessary when I am expected to be at the top of my game, but I am confused when it is called arrogance. I do not know how to fix my problems and cannot recognize my when I have made my family both immediate and

extended wish I would just stop. They say I
have been obsessed for the past few years,
digging in family business and causing
others great pain by remembering the
ugliness of our history. I expect to be
ostracized, although being alone is my
greatest fear.

PART IX

IS IT POSSIBLE TO CHANGE THE DIRECTION
OF MY LIFE WITHOUT CONSIDERING THAT
THERE ARE OTHER OPTIONS? WHO DO I SEE
WHEN EVERYONE LIKE ME SAYS, "SHHH BE
QUIET, IT WILL GO AWAY," EVEN THOSE WHO
HAVE MY PAIN WARN ME TO BE QUIET AND DO
NOT TELL ANYONE. I TRIED UNSUCCESSFULLY
TO KEEP IT IN BUT I COULD NOT, IT HURT
TOO MUCH, BUT NO ONE BELIEVED ME, SO IS
CHANGING THE HUSH AROUND THE PAIN
POSSIBLE?

CHAPTER 17

*It's about realizing, painfully, you've
kept that voice inside yourself, locked away
from even yourself. And you step back and
see that your jailer has changed faces. You
realize you've become your own jailer.*
—Tori Amos

Trust Destroyed

In the summer of 1979, I would learn
what the remainder of my childhood had in
store for me. "Look," he said, my brother,
who was tall and handsome even as a young
teenager, who I idolized, he was surely my
big brother who was cute and smart. He and
my other brother who was not quite as tall
but nothing could take away the fact that he
was what you just call fine. He was a
teenager that had more girls than he could
handle and those beautiful curly locks of
his made you want to just look at him. Both
wore perfect afros and many of the girls in
middle school and high school could only
wish they would say hello. Their fame and

glory only lasted between the hours they got on the bus until they returned home where they became nothing, as we all did when we returned.

Nevertheless, at eight years old I was happy that my brothers were cute and actually talking to me! Not like a little kid, but like I was important. They wanted to show me some pictures in secret and they could only show me if they could trust that I would be quiet. I was eight years old and knew that they never spent time with the "kids," they were practically grown to me, they had two numbers for their ages, and I was only eight. I was getting ready to go to the second grade. So it was really nice for them to talk to me a "chap" that was still playing outside in the dirt, but I was getting ready to go and they were going to give me some secrets on how to survive. That night they came and asked me if I wanted to

see something magical and pretty. I was
more than eager, I felt downright honored
that they wanted to show me something. They
only had one rule and if it had been that I
had to act like a monkey, I would have done
it because I felt special. There rule
however was that I not tell anyone else, no
one could know; it was a secret and they
chosen me because I was special. Oh did I
feel special it was like someone telling me
that I was pretty or that I could bring a
book home or even get a book.

    We went in the back of the shed (or
work building) where no one could see and
they had these cool pretty pictures of girls
with long dresses, and pretty hats and make
up on their faces. We didn't have a
television so this was like having a
magazine and seeing what real people wore
and how the pretty people dressed. I thought
they were just beautiful, especially the

girl with the red dress, shoes, hat and all the feathery ruffles. Red was my favorite color, and still is and I was drawn to the girl in the red dress. They asked, "Do you think she is pretty?" "Yeah she is real pretty." "Do you want to look like her?" he asked. Yeah, but I cannot look like that, I ain't pretty I'm just a plain old ugly girl. "Well let us show you what she does to look like that, lift up this plastic." Eager and without hesitancy I lift the plastic expecting to find a regular girl who was plain like me and somehow did something special that I could do to look as beautiful as the first picture. What I found was the same girl in the red dress, with the red hat and red shoes, without her red feathery hat and her long flowing white hair hanging around her shoulders, with a red bra and red panties on and her red high heel shoes. The rest of her milky white skin was uncovered for anyone to see. Her arms, her neck, her stomach, her long, long legs were all uncovered. A look of amazement and fear encapsulated me, but I did not know why, I just knew that I was going to be in trouble. Nevertheless, I could not stop admiring how she had on clothes and then she did not, and how she was still smiling and not a bit shamed. My curiosity got the best of me because although I was embarrassed and ashamed I ask if they could do it again. I wanted to know how she could be dressed up and then look like she was just getting ready to dress up. It was magic to me and again I wanted to know how they learned to do magic with people.

    The trouble I thought I would be in was far from the real trouble that changed my life. I knew I was not suppose to see grown people with no clothes or just in underwear, I did not even wear a bra and had never seen a white naked person so I was in deep trouble if anyone found out. Trust me I was not about to get a beating for seeing naked people. My exposure to nakedness was limited to my sisters who were all older than me and I never thought about them getting dressed. They let me do it again and although I was scared, I was also excited because I just learned a special trick from my big brothers. My heart raced my flight or fight instincts kicked in but after the second time I did not want to see anymore and asked if I could go play now. Both of them looked at me as if they needed to tell me something important. "Allie you can go play but remember don't tell nobody and tomorrow we got a better trick to show you, it is not like today it is in the woods, we will get you when we get it all ready." At eight years old I was nervous and excited at the same time, I didn't want to see no more

white ladies whose dresses came off like
paper dolls, but they must have a play house
in the woods and it's a secret that they
want to share with me. I quickly forgot
about the girl with the red hat, red dress,
red high-heeled shoes and the milky white
skin, but I could only dream about the
secret playhouse that would be in the woods.
I loved my brothers and was glad they wanted
to show me their special place.

Part X

I CANNOT HIDE HOW ASHAMED I WAS WHEN
THEIR EYES LOOKED ON MY NAKED SKIN, WHEN
THEIR HANDS TOUCHED MY SMALL CHESTS, AND
MY BACK TOUCHED THE EARTH, BUT MOSTLY
WHEN THE EYES OF THOSE I LOVED SO MUCH
MADE TEARS STREAM DOWN MY FACE.

CHAPTER 18

She couldn't get any farther away inside from her skin. She couldn't get away.
—Cynthia Voigt

The First Time

All day I waited while we picked up the trash and other stuff that was all over the yard, played with my other brothers and sisters, while they went with my father somewhere. All day I waited for them to come for me and show me their secret. Finally, late in the afternoon, they got back and I was playing nothing particular just outside because we were not allowed inside except to eat and sleep. I noticed they had returned and anxious and excited I tried not to appear too eager but I was ready to go see what exciting adventure awaited me. However, they started doing stuff and because I was told not to tell anyone or say anything I thought they forgot about the surprise or changed their minds, or maybe got in trouble while they were out, so I did not say anything, I just anxiously waited for whatever would happen. After we ate supper, my father told us to get out of his face and go play somewhere. We usually went down in the woods where the creek was and while I was on my way with everybody else, they finally ran and got me.

I was "oober excited." "You didn't tell nobody about yesterday did you, cause if you did daddy is gonna give you a whooping? He knows and he said it is okay but you can't go blabbing your mouth to nobody. You still want to see the surprise we got for you today don't you." I shook my head vigorously in the affirmative and one of them grabbed my arm and said hurry up before anyone else sees you, and we ran in the opposite direction of everyone else. We got to a spot in the woods, but nothing was there but trees, leaves, briars, and the

regular stuff that is in woods. I asked,
"Where is the surprise?" "You remember the
girl in red don't you?" "Yeah." "Well we
didn't show you everything yesterday there
is two more sheets to lift do you want to
see them?" With an uneasy feeling in my
stomach, I slowly and disappointingly
nodded. I really wanted to see the playhouse
and forget about the girl with the red dress
and milky white skin; I wanted to play, but
I guess this is part of the surprise. We all
sat down on the bare ground and the leaves
scratched the part of my legs that extended
from the cutoff pants turned into shorts
that I wore. They took the picture out and
asked me if I wanted to take the first
plastic off again, reluctantly and without
anticipation, I slowly took the plastic off
and the woman was again in her red panties,
red bra and red shoes. Appearing nonchalant,
they said we were going to play a fun game

with the woman and the picture. Bewildered yet finally excited that this must be the surprise "a new game" that wasn't for everybody else. The rules were simple but the fear it elicited within my being was indescribable. They said that we were to pretend we were like the woman and could take off our plastic one sheet at a time. I must have appeared confused and thus they clarified that our plastic was our real clothes. My stomach began to hurt and I did not want to be there anymore. "I want to go home, I don't want to see no more," I said. "It's too late you can't daddy said we have to do it today."

Tears streamed slowly down my face as confusion and helplessness set in. There was the reality that I was scared of my father, who was really tall and he hit really hard, and the thought of taking my clothes off in front of boys outside in the woods just seemed wrong. Unsure on all fronts I decided not to leave because what if they told and I got a whooping, so I did not leave. Both of them took their shirts and shorts off and stood in front of me with just their underwear on, shamed I turned around and then I heard, "Now it's your turn." I had on a really dirty week worn dingy red clay filled shirt and even dirtier shorts. The tears that came down my face no longer streamed they flooded and my stomach felt like a hurricane was churning in the very epicenter of my gut. They just stood there becoming impatient with my "stupid baby crying" and more forcefully told me to go ahead and take off my shirt and shorts because they had and nothing happened. I was already ashamed of my nakedness because unlike my sisters I was neither thin nor very pretty, I was always described using the adjectives "fat and cute" and with a personality that exuded lack of confidence and "wimp" as I was also called, shame overtook me. As I took off my shirt and my shorts, the floodgates that held my tears to a drizzle opened and I simply cried and cried and cried as I tried to cover up my overweight short body.

Standing there in my dirty underwear, I kept my head down not wanting to see myself or those without clothes, fear and embarrassment and shame controlled my cognition. I did not want to look at them and yet I felt their eyes staring at me without noticing my emotional turmoil, they just stared at me. "Okay, I will turn the next page," said my brother and as he did my eyes must have looked like golf balls because of the shocking image that was held up for me to see. With tears flowing from my eyes and no sounds, they showed me the woman standing naked with all of her milky white

skin showing. "Now we all have to take off
everything. You have to go first this time
cause we did last time." Unable to see
through the flood of tears and snot that was
coming from my facial orifices I said, "I
don't want to." "We gonna tell daddy if you
don't, and if he does it, it will be worse."
I slowly began to take my dirty panties off
crying uncontrollably, not because of what
would happen but because I was ashamed of
being naked and afraid of my father. I did
not know what he would do but I did not want
a whooping. I stood in the woods completely
naked with nothing to protect me from the
sky seeing my nakedness or the trees, or the
leaves, or grass or my brothers and most
horribly myself. I never looked at my body
and only remember that the girls took baths
at the same time and the boys took baths at
the same time, but I had never seen my body
just standing in the open naked, nor had I

ever seen a boy's body and did not look up
to see my brother's.

"Stop crying ain't nobody did nothing
to you yet," said one of them, "there is one
more picture and then we gonna show you how
to do everything." He raised the last piece
of plastic, which revealed the creamy white
woman lying on a bed with a naked man on top
of her. At that point, without understanding
my crying went from silent flooding of tears
to this horrible sound that rang in my ears
from an unfamiliar voice filled with fear.
It seemed that just as quickly as the sound
rang out one of them covered my mouth with
their hands and threateningly told me to
shut up before forcefully pushing me down
onto the leaves. I escaped to the treetops
and watched the surreal images. Like the man
on the picture, one of them laid on top of
me. It wasn't just that he was on top of me
he put the thing that he peed out of inside

my pee hole and with my mouth closed by my other brother's hand he went in and out. The pain was so bad I screamed but nobody could hear me, finally he stopped and I thought it was over, but they just switched and it started again one holding me down and holding my mouth and one going in and out in and out, in and out. I was told again to shut up before they hit me, and then I was rolled onto my stomach and they went again, by now I was gone.

As I sat in the tree, I stopped feeling anything and just watched them. I sat in the tree and watched them put their bodies in mine but there were no more tears and no more fighting. I had no sense of time and cannot say how long this violation occurred but finally they finished and before letting my mouth go reminded me that if I tell anyone I would get a whooping. They quickly put their clothes on and left me in the woods naked, sore, bleeding, and alive. What did I do to them, what did they do to me, and why did they do this to me? I slowly let my mind rejoin my body and yet as I got up a numbness of mind made me feel almost robotic. I felt like I had returned from a mission of war with what I believed to be allies only to learn that they were the true enemy. I rationalized the events and could not recall how I had gone from looking at a pretty girl with milky white skin to sitting in a tree watching my body be torn apart. I hypnotically pulled on my dirty dusty panties, and red dirt clay filled shorts and food and soil stained shirt and started walking I was forced back into my body when with each step I felt the worst pain of my life. I thought I was going to die, tears continued to roll down my face as I took what seemed to be the long walk to the back of the house.

Everyone was out playing, including my two brothers. I could see my mother in the kitchen; I went into the kitchen where my mother was cooking and learned the one lesson that reigned true in my life for nearly eleven more years. Tears streaming down my face I choked through the words to tell her what happened and I vividly remember hearing these words back, "Go wash your face and go on back outside and go to play, this may have been the first time but it won't be the last."

CHAPTER 19

*Hope . . . which whispered from the
Black Box that records all. After all the
other plagues and sorrows had escaped, is
the best and last of all things. Without it,
there is only time. And time pushes at our
backs like a centrifuge, forcing outward and
away, until it nudges us into oblivion . . .
It's a law of motion, a fact of physics . .
. , no different from the stages of white
dwarves and red giants. Like all things in
the universe, we are destined from birth to
diverge. Time is simply the yardstick of our
separation. If we are particles in a sea of
distance, exploded from an original whole,
then there is a science to our solitude. We
are lonely in proportion to our years.*
—Ian Caldwell, *The Rule of Four*

The Box

Hope is our strength. It is why we
continue to exist. It is what we strive to
find when our world appears desolate, but an
ounce of strength remains. My Black box is
much like the black box of a plane where all
information is recorded, but if not
retrieved after the crash it also resembles

Pandora's Box.

Pandora's Last Words

    Pandora is one of the most recognized
Greek mythical characters. Pandora was the
first woman, created by Zeus. Upon her
creation, the gods gave her many gifts –
beauty, charm, wit, artistry, and
shrewdness; the last gift was curiosity. The
god also included a box, which she was told
ardently, not to open. Although she
possessed many great gifts, her gift of
curiosity could not be tamed, thus making
the one rule the most interesting part of
her existence. What could be in this box?
Why was it so important to keep it
restrained inside? She fought to obey the
command by attempting to bury the box deep
into the ground. However, the pull of
curiosity caused her to dig it up. Finally,
she could hold back no longer, she lifted

the lid, and out flew all the evils of the world, such as toil, illness and despair; yet not only were evils in the box at the bottom of the box lay hope.

Pandora was so frightened by what she saw; she wanted to close the box. Although she closed it, the evils could not be put back in, but neither was *hope*.

Allie's Black Box

Similarly, Allie was gifted with gifts I would rather not name, as they appeared often times to be the causes of the evils. My box full of pain that I had stuffed in so deeply until one more item would surely be the death of me. It always lurked in the recesses of my mind but I was too busy to focus on what was in it, for surely, if it was in the box it could not be good. Many times little pieces of information and memories would slip out via a television show or a conversation that I would trigger my memory of something in the box. I would and continue to be unable to cope with the memory and take it so seriously that it was no longer the program but me.

Hope did not seem to reside with me and to think about opening the box and reliving what I knew was unbearable pain was not an option. I was too busy being a "good mother, and a good wife" and "trying to be somebody by getting all the education I could." I could not fail at either of those jobs because it would be known that I was a worthless piece of chewed gum that had been stepped on and now cursed by the unfortunate one who had me on the bottom of their just purchased Italian Amedeo Testoni Loafers. Worthless, I accepted, being cursed I accepted; but failing to be a good mother and wife which I had seen neither was unacceptable.

Pandora's Box is so named because in Greek Mythology Pandora was created as the first woman, beautiful in all ways. She was created as a punishment to humankind. Zeus commanded Hermes to teach her to be deceitful, stubborn, and curious. Aphrodite gave her femininity, and Athena taught her great crafts. With all of her gifts and great beauty, Hermes took her to marry Prometheus brother who was responsible for the state of humankind. Although warned not to take gifts from the gods, Epimetheus could not overcome the vision that stood before him, and took Black as his wife. Again, as the legend goes Black's curiosity won the best of her and she opened the box of gifts that she received from the gods. When she opened the box all illness, hardship, and every evil thing started coming out of the box. Out of fear she tried to close the box and as she did so, some say hope was locked up inside.

I cannot say that I ever believed hope was in the box, only illness, hardship, pain, and all manner of evil because I placed it there. However, like Black I have opened the box. It appeared that only the evil that was pushed so far down into the box would emerge. However, I began to notice the box became less fearful and tolerable and I found that hope was not in my box, but that it was and is the box. How else could I bear the horrors of a life filled with abuse yet when I relive each incident as they are released I am terribly afraid of their reality, and yet once I look up and open my eyes and my heart, hope emerges and I am freed?

Part XI

A VICTIM IS DESPISED FOR HURTING,
TALKING, AND BEING VICTIMIZED; "IT WAS
NOT YOUR FAULT"," STOP HAVING A VICTIM
MENTALITY" WHICH IS IT? WHO IS THE
VICTIM? HOW LONG CAN VICTIMS HOLD THE
PAIN, THE HURT, OR THE MEMORIES IS IT
AN HOUR, A DAY, A MONTH, A YEAR BUT NOW
IT IS TIME "TO GET OVER IT…BUT
HOW"?

CHAPTER 20

Victims often apologize for wrongful acts perpetrated on them by others, releasing the perpetrator and re-victimizing themselves.

- PGHG

"To Feel or Not to Feel…"

At the young and obviously tender age of eight years old it is difficult to know the difference between love, hate, and any other emotions that are naturally supposed to be embodied from parents to their offspring. All an eight-year-old can realistically comprehend is the fact that they are happy or sad, according to psychologist Jean Piaget, a well-respected contributor of modern and post-modern thought regarding the stages of development in children. According to Piaget as children develop between the ages of two and seven they are largely incapable of rationalizing all the sensory experiences that are impacting their very existence. Piaget called this stage pre-operational, and defined it as the inability of the child to make sense of the rational reasoning of others. He uses a Freudian term "ego" meaning that the child is very egocentric and takes normal and abnormal events as part of their being; caused by them and their responsibility, thus their fault.

For example when my two older brothers raped me, I naturally sought protection and comfort from my mother; however, I was greeted with retribution and zero compassion. As a young child although slightly older, I remember trying to understand her lack of concern and attributing it to the fact, that it must have been my fault. I embodied the act as something that I had asked for, caused, or been in some way responsible for and hearing the strange words "it won't be the last time" made me accept the act as normal and acceptable. This irrational thought did not disappear with age; it continues to possess my cognition with the belief that the things that go awry in my life or those around me are somehow my fault. This confusion has controlled my every move and caused me to obsessively apologize for something completely out of my control, such as the rain coming on a day when everyone wanted sunshine. It must be my fault.

It must be my fault; because surely no one would allow such unforgettable pain to happen to someone, they love? Yet, at forty-one years old I seem to be aware of the fact that love defined as a space to lay your emotions; both good and bad, on the shoulders, face, body, and heart of the object of your love. It has nothing at all to do with compassion, safety, protection, passion, affection, or nature, it is just a word to excuse and justify all wrong. I do not think I can take anymore love.

It is common knowledge that "Humpty Dumpty fell off the wall and could not be put back together again." It is so important that we recognize the loss of innocence can never be returned, renewed or revived from the trauma. We attempt to manage the symptoms that are revealed as depression, outrage, anger, isolation, and hate by medicating ourselves to avoid the constant memories that lie just behind our eyelids. Controlling our powerful brains by incapacitating the parts that feel, leaving us like zombies who are addicted to the substance and afraid of our reality. Trauma, remembered or triggered does not go away with a pill it is just masked so that every day is Hallow and if we happen to emerge from the mask someone quickly instructs us of how important it is not to be seen. "Let it go, the past is the past, you have survived, look at what you have accomplished, just look at it behind the mask, don't tell anyone because they might judge you." I must be quiet about being unwanted from birth and sold to be enslaved, raped, beaten, battered, drugged, sodomized and berated worse than the dust that follows a plowing tractor and wear my mask and take my pills so I don't dredge up the past. The place I live without my mask is frightening, and it appears in the dark of the night or the light of the day, but I must put on the good mask. I must not feel, and surely, I must not allow the rain behind my eyelids to be seen by anyone, so I hide in the closet when the mask does not work. They cannot find me there and I cannot stop the tears from falling or explain why they are falling, so I run and run and run until my mind and body are so exhausted that I have no feelings. The race I run can never be won, because there is a past that always runs just behind me and I cannot make it go away without the pills.

Innocence cannot be purchased; it arrives at conception and can be destroyed before birth by those who are assigned by the sheer accident of birth to guard and protect you. Intervention is always a day late and a dollar short. No one intervenes until innocence and the laughter that comes with being a child is long gone.

Maybe innocence is unclear, as William B. Yates stated, *"The innocent and the beautiful have no enemy but time."* As a young girl, I believed in the beauty of life, all life, trees, sky, moon, grass, people, and most of all myself. I felt that I could do anything my brothers did especially the three I was closest in age with. We were closer in age a year sometimes

and not quite a year for my older brother
and me, so I wanted to be as rough and tough
as they were. If they climbed a tree and
jumped down, I wanted to climb to the next
highest branch and jump to prove that I
could do anything they could. Two acres of
yard therefore would play together in the
woods. It was especially imperative that if
someone turned into the driveway all signs
of children must run to the forest. No one
ever saw the children because if anyone came
to our home all of the children had to run
to the forest to avoid a beating; therefore,
we learned to make the forest our primary
playing area. "Being seen and not heard" was
not the motto of our home it was "I don't
want to see you or hear you unless I call
you."

When this lesson is embodied, it
teaches isolation; physically and
emotionally, it shuts down dialogue and

opens up the door to enslavement and mind control. Ultimately, it engenders a sense of self-deprecation, where no one has to belittle you or tell you are worthless, you are quite capable of ensuring that everyone knows. None of the institutional capital acquired diminishes the poor self-image that seems is always lurking just below the thin layer of your epidermis waiting to be punctured. Ensuring that you do not think highly of yourself regardless of the degrees you have earned, and the great children you have reared, and wonderful marriage you have held onto for more than twenty years. The embodiment of your worthlessness supersedes every accomplishment and always makes me ask the question "what am I living for?"

If the car breaks down you are very aware that although you were nowhere near it that you did something stupid and you are the one responsible for whatever goes wrong in your world and those you love. Therefore, I spend my life trying to repair all of the broken pieces for others as I continue to become more and more fragile and weak. I know I must apologize and hope for forgiveness but even that comes with a cost. My personal debts are so insurmountable that finding a way out of this maze of guilt is futile. Although it is irrational, my critical voice, the only one I have, only recalls what I have learned and the actions and reactions that were critical to my sanity as a child. I am not sure if the critical condemning voice can be minimized or shut off, I will let you know as I continue in therapy to try to shut it off.

What did I do?

I did not know until my brothers raped me that I was not like the boys; I was different from them in a major way. The fear that came with that knowledge seemed to change me in a way that was not the way I expected. The concept of fear with need seemed to become my coping mechanism. I could not fight, therefore I disappeared into my own head and went on many journeys until there was no feeling just expectation and almost anticipation with an incomprehensible yearning. I know it was my fault because as time passed, I did not understand that sex was not my choice, that being beat was abnormal, and at that time I did not even know that I was being sold, just that I was sent away a lot.

I learned to be afraid of what boys could do after the rape because I knew that as my mother said I would have to get used to being raped and I did (she was right). I stopped playing in the trees and was less interested in going deeply into the woods with my brothers. After the first incident, I was left alone for a while. I thought this meant that I was safe, that I was not the right type or something. I did not know that I was being bartered. Yes, bartered, sold for a few dollars and back breaking work to live with a lady that I had never seen before.

Part XII

THERE IS A HOUSE WHERE NO CHILD SHOULD
LIVE, IT IS LOCATED ON EVERY CONTINENT,
IN EVERY COUNTRY, AND EVERY
NEIGHBORHOOD; THE CHILD IN THAT HOUSE IS
A SLAVE AND CANNOT BE SAVED UNLESS THEY
RUN FAST, NO REALLY FAST, AND HIDE,
JUST DON'T LET THEM FIND YOU, THEY WILL
SEND YOU AWAY AGAIN!

CHAPTER 22

The housemaster's treatment of slaves
includes work expectations of an adult
servant. It is called a restavek, which in
Creole means child slave. The work is
arduous and the hours are long. The food and
clothing are just enough to meet basic
needs. The attic is locked every night.
Play, friends, not allowed.
- Anonymous

The Log Cabin

I remember one autumn my father telling

me to get in the car without explanation and

of course, I asked no questions. Like Black

my curiosity got the best of me, I was

extremely curious about why I had to go with

him, and nobody else did but I not dare ask,

no whipping today, so I went into my head. I

did wonder why a few of my dingy clothes

were in a trash bag in the car. Did I do

something wrong again, I did not tell

anymore, why am I going somewhere? Before

long or maybe it was longer than I thought,

but the time I spent in my head seemed to

whiz by. He pulled into the long dirt driveway, I saw the little green and white log cabin with the huge front yard, and then I heard the massive bark of a dog tied to a tree to the left of the little house. It was a German shepherd and his teeth were long and pointy, he was black and brown and around him there was no grass, only a couple of metal buckets, on his neck there was a chain that he pulled strongly against as he barked. I was very afraid of the dog and wondered, "who lives here and why is my father bringing me here." Then I saw her, an average size dark complexion woman came out of the front door and stood on the porch and spit something dark and black out of her mouth. She was the darkest person I had ever seen and she was what I thought of as fat at that time. She appeared to be eating but I could not guess what since one of her jaws was full of something that she kept spitting out into the yard.

My father sat in the car at the end of her long cemented walk to her front steps. I was told to gather my things because I would be staying there for a spell. The closer she came the uglier she was to me. Almost scary, so when she said with a gruff voice "come on in, bring your things in here and you can put them up in a minute" out of her mouth full of black stuff. I looked at my father who said "get on out you gonna be staying here for a while to help your cousin Laverne out, she needs someone to help her keep things up."

I numbly followed his and her instructions but knew that I could not cry because if I did I was going to get into more trouble. I did not know what I had done to make him give me away again, but I was really sorry and if I knew what it was I

would never do it again. Maybe it was what
had happened with my brothers, maybe I was
in trouble for telling my mother and she
told on me and now I have to live with this
ugly, fat woman who spits black stuff out of
her mouth and talks hard, not kind like many
girls but hard, like the angry dog that was
still barking. As soon as I got my stuff
out she went to the car and they talked for
a while.

What Makes a Slave?

I learned quickly that this was not a
vacation, not that I knew what a vacation
was but it definitely was not what I was
here for. As I walked down that long
sidewalk I noticed an engraving that showed
the name of the man whom I presumed had once
lived there. I approached this home and with
my brown paper grocery bag I held my things
tightly and once arriving at the steps where
I was only a few feet from the door, I

turned and looked to see if this was real, was I being left here alone with this woman. Was she behind me? What did she give my father and what were they saying? Maybe it was just for the weekend, maybe he made a mistake and this was not the right house; please don't let this be the right house. In the distance I hear the loud ruckus bark of the dog, I look to my left and notice the huge German shepherd again howling at me as if I would be his dinner. Afraid, terribly afraid of dogs, I cringed and walked up the three steps. I do not enter the house until she gets back to the porch and insists that I go in.

As I open the screen door it creeks as if it needed to be oiled or just changed. I open the next door and feel the warmth of the room but smell the oldness of the house and an odor that I am not familiar with but that causes me to gag. I stop, waiting for further direction and am told in a harsh tone to go on into the kitchen and the steps to the room are in the corner on the right. Startled I walk a little more briskly not focusing on the surroundings or the wall or the smells only that I was stuck with only my bag in this house with this lady. Why? What did I do wrong, why did they send me away? I went in as instructed so I would not get in trouble, but I was scared to go into the attic. I had lived upstairs and been locked in before, but timidly I looked behind me and saw the large black ugly woman who looked to be smiling but who sounded loud and harsh "go on take that bag on up to the attic, that's where you will be staying while you're here."

Aside: *It is Tuesday, December 7, 2010. I am awakened from a fitful and terrifying nightmare. I am at the house and locked in the attic. I have to go* *to the restroom and am utterly afraid to get out of bed. There is no restroom, there but my husband who hears me weeping awaken me and with sheer love in his voice tries to convince me that I am home and that I could go safely to the bathroom in our master bedroom. Quite unsure, very dazed and confused I am afraid and begin to cry, I hear the dog that we do not have, but that is outside of the cabin I have just been taken to live. I muffle my tears so she does not hear me. But why am I there? Why did he leave me? What did I do that was so bad that I have to go live in this scary place? The dog keeps barking and I have to go to the bathroom. Kindly, my husband arises from his slumber and walks with me gingerly as I am confused about my location at 2:00 AM. Along the*

way he assures me that I am home . . .
my house, not the attic, there is no
dog, and he will protect me. "This is
…; I love you, and will protect you.
You are safely at your home." After
finally using the bathroom, and washing
my hands, I feel somewhat comforted
with the idea, but all of the doors are
closed. What if this is a trick, what
if I really can't get out, what if they
are locked and he is just part of my
nightmare? I softly beg him not to hurt
me and ask if I can see if the door is
open. He tiredly says yes and watches
as I tip toe to the door afraid that
she might hear me trying to open the
door and I will get in trouble. I reach
for the doorknob with my right hand and
hold it quietly with my left so that it
does not make any noise. Once the door
is open, I am aware that I am home.

Living with the lady, whom I was to address as *Grandma*, caused me to feel sick and grateful at the same time; sick just to have to address her at all, and grateful that she was not my actual grandmother. I shyly took my brown grocery bag of clothes upstairs to a one-room space that was approximately a 10x10 space with a small twin size bed and a narrow chest of drawers which sat adjacent to the steps with the bed on the opposing wall. I sat on the bed and looked out the small 4x4 window and watched my father and the lady talking before he sped off without so much as a goodbye, a beep of the horn or anything close to an I Love You. Tears streamed down my face and loneliness once again was my only friend, as I looked around the eggshell painted space with brownish vinyl tile flooring and walls where boxes of stuff leaned. Before I could wallow in the feelings that whaled up inside me, or examine my new space, I heard "Girl get down here. There is stuff that got to be done." At seven years old I quickly, wiped the tears from my eyes and the snot from my nose with the sleeve of my shirt and went down the flight of steps into the kitchen where she stood waiting. My eyes red from the sea of tears, and yet clear enough to see that she was more unattractive than I had thought. I would soon learn that ugly was the least of my fears.

On that Saturday morning *Grandma* had a full list of work that needed to be completed before the day ended and I quickly learned that much of it would be my responsibility. "Girl go back yonder and get that rake out the shed, that front yard need to be raked, go on, *and better not see a leaf when you finish*, and it better not take all day." I must not have walked quickly enough because I heard "Girl if you don't get on out of here now, and do what I told you, I'm gonna get that belt and I betcha you will move a lot faster." I quickly moved toward the back door, found the rake lying against the shed, and walked around the left side of the house to the front yard. Standing at the corner of the yard the very breadth of the yard became so overwhelming, tears began to come fill my eyes, but just before the first one had a chance to touch my cheek I saw *Grandma* on the porch waiting for me. She pointed past the driveway showing me where to begin. To avoid hearing her scream at me again I quickly went to the area where she pointed. The yard was massive and so full of grand oak trees of all sizes; there were so many that I did not see the grass until several strokes of raking. The very thought of raking the huge yard was more than I could imagine my seven-year-old shoulders managing. I never raked anything in my life before, and began to use the tool like a broom. However, unlike a broom, the leaves would stick in the prongs of the rake and I would have to stop often to clean the rake so that it would work. I began raking and quickly piles of leaves began to dawn the yard like anthills on the side of a clay dirt filled yard. The vast amount of leaves that were in the yard, the sheer magnitude of the yard made my labor arduous and seem never ending.

Thirsty, tired, and hungry I began to slow down my pace. I wandered what was she doing and why did I have to rake the yard, and why couldn't I eat until I finished. I did not have any tears left to bleed from my eyes and yet I was too afraid to ask for even a drop of water. Therefore, I continued to rake the enormous yard and after what seemed like one hundred years, she trudged out the door with big black garbage bags heading in my direction. "Girl makes sure you get all of them piles up and remember there better not be a leaf left on this ground when you finish. Put them in these bags and take them over to the woods (pointing to the other side of the driveway) and empty them." Quietly and full of fear, I said, "Yes ma'am and can I have some water please?" She pointed to the front of the house and screamed, "The hose pipe is right there, you can get some water out of it, and make sure you turn that water all the way off when you finish." "Yes ma'am." She walked off and I began putting the piles of leaves into the bag until she went into the house. Then I went to the hose pipe which was attached to the house near a flower garden and drank water as if my body were a desert being honored by the gods with a rain shower that only comes once every one hundred years. Of course I over did it and my stomach begin feeling as if someone were forcing their feet into the side of my stomach trying to let out the water. I knew not to complain because I would be in trouble if the leaves were not cleaned up. From the time I arrived and picked up that rake until nearly sundown I worked in that front yard raking, gathering, and emptying bags of leaves. I would look at the yard at times and try to make a game out of the task; for example how big can I make a pile or can I put a whole pile in one trash bag. As silly as these internal competitions were they helped the arduous task to move more quickly. Finishing would be by moonlight, but I found myself no longer aware of the work but relishing in the beauty of the leaves and trees. I began naming the trees and challenging myself to remember all of them for there were many. As I think back,

I do not know when the anguish turned into pleasure just that it did.

Eventually, I looked around to find that I had completed the task and now must pray that I did a good job. I slowly walked to the front porch where she was sitting and said timidly "I finished getting the leaves up." Standing to observe and walking to the assigned area along with checking the location I was to take the leaves she said "you don't see these sticks that you left and you didn't put them in the woods, next time walk past that tree over yonder and put them leaves." Hungry and tired I thought my work was done and that I would be greeted with food.

I learned soon that work was my purpose for being there and work I would always do. Once in the house she instructed me to wash my face and hands and go peel some potatoes, and chop some onions and celery for potato salad for Sunday dinner. If I was hungry, she said there were beans in the refrigerator, and some cornbread on the stove. Although I hated beans and there was nothing worse than cold beans, I ate doggishly as if it was my last meal. I was so hungry that I ate multiple "helpings" of the food before she noticed that I had not begun the assigned work. "You done ate your days' worth by now and probably tomorrow's too, now hurry up and get them taters peeled." I quickly began peeling potatoes, chopping onions, and cutting celery as she flitted around the kitchen doing other preparations for the Sunday meal. I had never done this task before and of course, I did a poor job, ended up getting a whooping, and sent up to bed. Upstairs I prayed that I could go home the next day, but the next day did not come for a long time. That was one of many nights I have cried myself to sleep because life was hopeless and all I could do was pray to die for there was no hope for me.

During my stint of living with *Grandma (which I never felt comfortable saying),* she exposed me to several new experiences that were pleasurable and became embedded in my memory as "fun." The first was during many of the summer months she would wake up and decide to go fishing, being the tomboy little girl that I had been with my brothers made this experience more than about catching an unsuspecting fish, but it was a moment of freedom from work. We would get up early (she said she wanted to get there before it got too hot and find a good shaded spot) and make bologna and cheese sandwiches, pack potato salad in a bowl, put some lemonade in a "big mouth mason jar" and finally if it was a really good day she would put a piece of cake in there too. I loved the preparation, and did not have any problem with getting up early, because the day was going to be so much fun. We would set out on foot and walk a short distance down the road that she lived off and head through the woods to a pond surrounded by trees and other foliage. When the moment hit her she would say "This is it, this is where we gone fish from today." I did not understand what made one spot better than another and frankly, it did not matter; I just loved the idea of being in nature. I was never afraid to bait a fishing hook, in fact, I loved touching the cold earthworms that we had gotten from the yard the day before or she had picked up from one of the country stores. They felt gushy and squiggled in my hands and tickled my palms. Sometimes they would break in two parts, but I thought it was cool because they still seem to move as if they were whole.

In addition to fishing, every summer she would go to Georgia to visit her sister. The trip was *long* but again it was an adventure and was amazingly fun. With a car packed with chicken, and all of the previously mentioned treats, (from the fishing trip) we would set off in her big American made vehicle headed on a journey. I did not know where we were going but this experience was one that put eyes on a world beyond measure. The landscape went from the hills and grass in most of Virginia, to the flat land and sand of South Carolina, to the swampy, muggy ecosystem of coastal Georgia. There were big houses, trailer parks, apartments, farms with all types of livestock. I escaped into each of their worlds; I imagined how the people in many of the houses lived. Of course they did not have to wash baseboards or rake yards, or live in attics they only had perfect lives.

Children who appeared to be close to my age were playing outside, laughing and running freely, I imagined running with them until my thoughts were interrupted by a question or directive. Everything seemed to be just perfect, their homes, parents and their laughs. In my fantasy world, I had perfect parents who dressed me in pretty dresses with my hair in ponytails hanging loosely down my back.

It was at this home that I was introduced to God's most amazing creation. During the autumn season we would go to the West Virginia Mountains and the fear and thrill of driving on the edge of the world were equally dominating my conscious. I had never been to a mountain, but my nature was to meld with the natural décor of the earth. I was the kind of girl who wanted to get on the cliff and imagine being able to fly high in the air like the eagles, or climb the highest tree and snuggle on a branch. I admired the sheer height, breadth and magnitude of being so high up and feeling like no one else existed. I do not know why we went there, but I developed a lifelong love affair with the mountains. Although I must honestly admit that at times my stomach would get that nervous shaky feeling because I was a bit unnerved by the deep valleys and the massive hills (mountains). Yet, I fell deeply in love with the very concept of huge trees, and little houses sitting in odd places as if any moment they would slide down the mountain into the chasm below. It was as if I was on top of the world and the only things higher were the birds that flew overhead, the trees and God. The vivid colors were so breathtaking that I became a part of their wonder and awe. It was like being in the midst of a rainbow and being able to touch every single color. I closed my eyes and lay in the leaves with my arms and legs stretched to make colorful leaf angels. The mesmerizing scene before me stretched wide, deep and oh so very high. It was sheer beauty, a million leaves with colors so amazing that the color prism could not duplicate them, when I can become a part of nature I will "ashes to ashes and dust to dust" no more jail for me. I am at peace when I am with nature and my wondering mind would place me in some role different from what my actual role was. I do not recall our purpose or who we went to see or what happened on the trip; I just remember the safety and beauty of the trees and the mountains that offered shelter and many caves in which to hide. I knew that the first chance I got in life to be free I would experience what my vivid imagination could only provide me a glimpse. Each autumn during the month of my birth, October, I spend as much time in the mountains as possible, and the feeling of peace, safety and serenity remains unscathed by time.

My birthday is during the greatest season of the year autumn where color rains from the branches of every leaf tree and fills the sky and earth with beauty. Until you have to rake the up of course. It had been a year since I moved in with my father's cousin and that time had arrived again where leaves bathed the yard. But this time I was excited for this October with my birthday on the horizon, I was asked if I wanted to have a birthday party. I had never had any kind of party and was excited about the thought of my day being celebrated. I was asked who I wanted to attend this gathering; and of course I said my brothers and sisters for I had not seen them in over a year. I excitedly called their names as if simply stating them made me feel their presence. However, my joy fizzled very quickly when I was informed that they could not come and that I needed to pick friends from school. As the words rolled off her dark lips that were filled with snuff that rested between her lower lip and her gums, anger arose in me that I could not mask. Angry and sad I quietly stated that I did not want a party if my brothers and sisters could not come. I had not seen them in nearly a year; even at Christmas and Thanksgiving, so I did not want anything for my birthday. I bowed my head and as I was scolded I became "Laural" inside my head and remember nothing but the tiny ants that crawled on the ground where my eyes were cast. I stood there determined not to feel or reveal my anger but played with the children in *Little House in the Big Woods* by Laural Ingalls Wilder (1932). This defiance was not lost on Grandma. No, she noticed my distant and unresponsive manner, and it did not go over well. To add fuel to the fire, I was barred from attending an upcoming school field trip that was the next week. I heard "Because you so hard headed and don't appreciated anything you won't be going on that school trip next week." I maintained my resolve, I was not surprised about the trip being taken, so I just stood there until I was sent out to pull grass out of the flowers and feed the dog.

Later in the week, my father came for one of his quick visits. He never got out of the car; he just pulled in and asked me if I was okay. "Yes, sir," I said. He asked if I needed anything and I told him that my school had a trip that was $3.00 but Ms. Laverne said she didn't have the money so I couldn't go. He pulled out his wallet and surprisingly gave me the money, which I quickly put into my pockets so she could not see it and walked away as she came toward the car. After a brief encounter and exchange, he left and she returned to the house. I stayed outside busying myself as long as I could before I was called in for supper. When I went back into the house, she said, "What you say to him?" Looking down so that I would not get smacked for looking a grown up in the face I said, "Nothing, I just answered his questions about was I all right and I told him yes."

The following day I paid for the trip with the three dollars I received from my father. Each day as the teacher reminded us to bring our lunch for the trip and to bring snacks. I knew I would not be able to bring lunch and just decided I would just say I forgot and that I was not hungry. When the day finally arrived for the trip, I decided to ask if I could take my lunch to school since my class would be on the trip. Not to be out witted she asked why I needed to take my lunch, not savvy at thinking of a good reason I just said, "The trip is today and my daddy gave me money to go when he came." I believed she was the boogie man and she became enraged, livid and began screaming, "I thought I told you, that you were not going on the trip, you think you slick don't you? Well you better enjoy it because when you get back you will get a whooping." She did not give me the lunch and told me to find my own lunch since I could find my own money.

Holding back tears, I went out and waited for the bus, determined not to act like anything was wrong "Laural" returned and I kept her with me all day. I decided I would thoroughly enjoy my trip and would avoid a whooping at the same time. Once at school, I told my teacher that I forgot to bring my lunch and she said that I could get some from the cafeteria and they gave me a brown bag with a peanut butter sandwich, milk and vegetable snacks. I do not remember where we went, but the trip was great and when we returned to school, I did something that would be my legacy for what appears to be a lifetime of seeking safety. I ran away.

We returned from the trip and without any thought of the possible consequences I got on the bus with my friend and that was that! I played, ran, and enjoyed my friend and her brothers and sisters who gave me a snack and let me play. I do not remember if anyone actually called but he showed up. When my friend's dad came home I think he called my father because not long after he came home my father pulled in the driveway. He thanked the family for letting me stay and once in the car asked was I supposed to be at their house? I told him about the trip and the whooping that was coming to me for

asking him for money for the trip. After
explaining what happened he did not fuss at
me or tell me I was getting a whooping. When
we got to the house, he just told me to go
out in the yard and play with the other
chaps.

After dark, I was in the back yard and
saw *Grandma's* car pull into the driveway,
fear engulfed me and I shivered as if I was
actually getting the whooping I had been
promised. I had worried all day that I would
have to go back and although I was supposed
to be playing with my brothers and sisters a
feeling of complete fear that I could not
shake consumed my very breath and paralyzed
my body. When I heard the car slow and then
heard the gravel, scream beneath the tires
of the long 1978 Buick. We were not allowed
to be in sight of visitors or in hearing
range of our parents but I couldn't help it.
I hid and waited just at the edge of the

chimney on the side of the house, with my stomach in a series of knots so tight I had to bend with my knees in my chest just to stop the cramps. I heard the car stop and Ms. Laverne walked onto the porch and spoke to my father who was standing at the edge of the porch leaning on the porch railing. I listened for my name to be called and I knew I would have to return to the place of horror, to the attic, and worse of all get a whooping. Although I knew I was not supposed to be near the house when a car pulled in the driveway I could not make myself move and squatting down on the side of the house with my knees in my chest, I listened intently to the conversation. I could not make out the words that were said but only heard the muttered sounds of an agitated conversation that ended with *Grandma* spinning wheels and making the gravel scream in pain as she sped out of the yard, and no further words were spoken to me regarding the situation. I never returned to the green, black and white log cabin.

Part XIII

THERE IS A PHRASE, "THE ELEPHANT IN THE
LIVING ROOM", WHICH PURPORTS TO
DESCRIBE WHAT IT'S LIKE TO LIVE WITH A
AN ABUSER. PEOPLE OUTSIDE SUCH
RELATIONSHIPS WILL SOMETIMES ASK, "HOW
COULD YOU LET THIS GO ON FOR SO MANY
YEARS? DIDN'T YOU SEE THE ELEPHANT IN
THE LIVING ROOM?" AND IT'S SO HARD FOR
ANYONE LIVING IN A MORE NORMAL SITUATION
TO UNDERSTAND THE ANSWER THAT COMES
CLOSEST TO THE TRUTH; "I'M SORRY, BUT
IT WAS THERE WHEN I MOVED IN. I DIDN'T
KNOW IT WAS AN ELEPHANT; I THOUGHT IT
WAS PART OF THE FURNITURE."

-STEPHEN KING

CHAPTER 23

*Home, House or Shelter; which protects
from fears, wipes the tears, and warms the
soul; not a building with rooms where doors
are locked and tears are shed in silence,
and pain has no comforter.*

Home Again

I arrived home at the end of third
grade and changed schools for the third time
returning from Albright School to Milliken
School. Having started school at Stanley
Elementary in a small rural community and
only being in the third grade, changes were
just a part of the process. Friends were not
an option therefore; it was just another
place to get the same information. Attending
Milliken school was fun. I had great
teachers at all of my schools and they are
the reason I pursued the field of education,
not to teach, but to give hope to those who
felt they had no hope. At Milliken school I
was in classes with regular kids learning

what fourth-graders learn, and because school was relatively easy for me or not important, I did not spend too much time thinking about the work, but focused my attention on the relationships; both girls and boys. I wanted to be normal and fit in; at home, I was a part of the clan that were farmers, workers, abuse victims and a nonissue, however at school I wanted to be somebody normal. I did not have to be popular, just normal, or at least have a friend. Therefore, I became friends with the people in my class and we would play on the playground together, enjoying kid games like kick ball, jump rope, hopscotch and other games that brought great pleasure and no pain. I knew the time would be limited but I hoped I would be able to enjoy one full year at a place where I could care about nothing, just run and have fun without pain.

My teachers always liked me and I always loved my teachers. I had Ms. Jenkins a tall thin white lady who was tough and smart. She seemed to be the fountain of knowledge and I wanted to drink as much knowledge as possible. I loved learning and could not get enough books to read. The library was and continues to be a favorite hangout spot for me. At Jackson elementary school, Ms. Garrett was my teacher and she was beautiful and smart too. She was a nice teacher and liked me and would strive to ensure my safety. After the trip fiasco and changing schools, the only thing I missed was my teacher.

Working Hard by Day and Night

In 1979 after returning home, I was unsure if I had made the right decision or not. During that year, things were different. My father was different. He was

still mean and working us hard and nothing
stopped with the abuses but he seemed to be
away from home more. I had never known him
to be gone for long periods of time or to
rest and seem simply tired. After sneaking
around and "listening to grown folks
conversations," we heard that he was going
to the doctor. I knew that we did not go to
doctors unless we were really, really sick
and that meant that "Black Draught",
Liniment, and other home remedies taken by
mouth could not make us well. After reading
up on these home remedies, they were
commonly used for horses, but I guess if
they could work for farm animals then we
were taking the right medicines. So for him
to be going to the doctor was confusing at
best. No child and not many grownups would
have asked "what is wrong, why do have to go
to the doctor." I cannot believe that we
would have gotten the usual "stay in a

child's place . . . and out of grown folks business" and if we did, it would be preceded or post ceded by a painful wallop that caught you off guard and knocked you and the wind out. We were children not idiots.

Therefore, we did what normal children who have "nose" problems do, we just happened to need water, or be playing outside near the window, or doing something close enough to hear but not be noticed or seen. Eventually, through the many ears that lived on the property and the conversations that often happened when "us chaps" were not "around" or at night we discovered out that he was sick. Not a little bit sick but a real bad off sick. He wasn't going to have nobody cutting on him, whatever he came here with he is going to die with. I nor my brothers or sisters knew the breadth of his kind of sick but we just knew it was bad.

Father's Last Year

Early in the spring of 1981, I remember us working in tobacco and on other people's farms more than ever before. We seemed to be trying to store up enough food for life. He worked on adding space to the small farmhouse that he had purchased a couple of years earlier and he was just different. He added two rooms to the back of the house for us kids to sleep in and a huge kitchen. The table had to be built inside the house because it needed to be big enough for all of us to eat together but a table that size was too big to buy or move so he built it inside with benches where it remained until the house was destroyed. He then added a back porch that took us all spring and summer to fill. We carried five or ten-gallon buckets of red clay dirt for months to fill the center of the porch and limit

the amount of concrete that would be needed
to close the structure.

We had hundreds of chickens in a
chicken coup in the backyard and pigs on the
right side of the house near the woods and a
goat tied to a tree and even an old pony.
The animals were great, we had often lived
where there were farm animals; some were
ours and some were the property owners, but
all of these were ours. In the summer we
would gather eggs and as the chickens
multiplied we would have chicken killing
days which were quite fun. We kids would
chase the chickens all over and when we
caught one my big brothers or father would
cut off its head and let it run around
headless until it stopped. We would pick it
up by its feet and take it to one of the
older boys or my father and they would put
it in a big giant black pot with boiling
water, take it out quickly, and give it back

to us. We would have the best part; we got to take all of the feathers off before giving it to my mother. Like the chickens the pigs had a time to be killed to, but they were big and fat. All spring and summer they ate slop and corn and the best of all was watermelon rinds. There is nothing more appreciated by a big fat pig than a watermelon. So after we had eaten them as far down as we were allowed, my mother would yell, "Don't eat the white part. It's gonna make your stomach sick." We would reluctantly stop eating but joyfully run to feed it to the pigs. They would chomp on those rinds like they had never eaten before and they would try to get them from each other, but we would through them all of the pig pin and whichever one got there first was lucky that day. In the fall just as it got really cold and before Thanksgiving, my father and brothers would get up really early and put on warm clothes and stocking hats and go outside, and we young'uns would watch as they put the shotgun right up to the pigs head and pulled the trigger. The thing we couldn't figure and still can't was that the dumb pigs just walked up to the guns like they was ready to be shot. Not like the chickens who ran from us, but they just walked right up to the gun. Most dumb thing ever was that after the first one was shot you would think the others would run; but they didn't, each one came like they knew that it was over. Work was daily, but it wasn't unusual it was normal and oftentimes fun because we were all together. We didn't get any special treats or anything for working but we all liked to talk and laugh so even while we were pulling tobacco, picking vegetables, chasing chickens or cleaning chitterlings we had fun.

Weekends were not a day off or a day on it just was another day. We went to the creek, that ran into the Dan River, that was deep in the woods behind our home about a quarter mile and brought buckets of water back for the ringer washer that was used to do laundry. Bucket after bucket for a million clothes and everything was bleached and hung on the clothesline near the well that was used to only get drinking water if the pipes froze and ran using a pump into the house to cook with. We made lye soap for washing our bodies and worked nonstop to make sure everything was clean and in its proper place. Yearly we would get a truckload of sand dropped in the back yard, not to play in, but to scrub all of the pots and pans that were used for meals. My father did not want to see a single black piece of crud on any of the pots or pans when we finished. Work, yes, but also fun. That summer was filled with activity, and we barely noticed that my father was getting thinner and did more instructing than doing.

Sundays were rest days, we would be able to play all day unless we were caught sitting too close to the adults, then we would have to "pick up the yard." Every piece of trash or item that was not supposed to be in the yard had to be gotten up, and on two plus acres with nineteen children there was lots to pick up. My mother kept the front yard filled with blooming plants and bushes, so we were not allowed to play in that area but the back yard was a free zone and we made everything a toy from old cans to bottles, sticks, bicycle rims, tobacco sticks, and twine. We would take twine and roll it to make a ball and play jack rocks with rocks, or use an old ball and play basketball after attaching the bicycle rim to the light pole. Cowboys and

Indians was always a weekend event and with
bow and arrows made of stick and strings,
guns for the cowboys that were sticks, and
even horses for both derived from sticks
there was no lack of imagination just time.
If the big June Bugs or Beetles were out we
would catch them and tie a string around
their leg and let them fly like a kite, or
trap lightening bugs and catch butterfly's,
no creepy crawler got a free ride.
Earthworms broken to see how they kept
moving, grasshoppers legs removed to see if
they could still hop, and even daddy long
legs would lose their legs to see if their
body could move. An adventurous and untamed
mind led us into an imaginative world where
nothing was off limits, wild blueberries,
blackberries, wild strawberries, persimmons,
all tasty treats even black cherries that I
hated. Rest day usually ended up being a
trouble day because somebody was going to

get hurt and go tell and then we would all
have to come back to the house if we were in
the woods or playing far from home. The
woods were the most fun; we would plant the
beans that my mother did not use when she
was preparing dinner and any seeds we could
find to make our own garden. We would play
Tarzan and Jane by swinging on the branches
across the creek, and see who could climb
the highest in the tree. This was my
favorite. Climbing then and now brings me
great joy.

During this year of work until you drop
beatings, molestation and withholding of
food continued, but because it was expected
it was not worth thinking about. That summer
I received my worst beating ever for an
infraction that even today I cannot recall.
I remember five of us who were all close in
age seven to ten were playing near the woods
in the back of our house. We often played

near an entry or path that was created as a
result of many children walking the same
path many times during any given day. There
was what we called the "trash hole" which
was a huge hole dug out in the far right
corner of our back yard and about the
30x40x25 filled with garbage. Just in front
of the "trash hole" and near the entry path
to the woods was the outhouse that all of
the kids had to use. We had the option of
the outhouse or the woods and frankly, the
woods smelled better and the flies were not
as bad. We were all in this general area
because we often found treasures in the
trash hole to play games with; I was the
only girl in the age group. Something did
not go the way one of the younger brothers
wanted it to and he ran crying to the front
yard and told my father that I had done
something to him. As I sated I cannot
remember what my crime was but I immediately

called to the front porch. I do not know if I was asked if I had done what I was accused of only that I was slapped so hard that I fell to the ground. While on the ground I was kicked many times as if I were a football and in kicking practice. My father was spouting expletives and rules that I could not understand. I zoned out and rolled up into a ball for protection, when that did not work; I rolled under the cream-colored Chevy truck that parked close to the front porch to shield myself from the battery. I recalled my father getting in the truck and backing it up without concern that he may actually kill me. I lay curled up on the ground in the center front of the truck and once the truck had backed off me I got up and ran as fast as my short legs could take me into the woods on the left side of our house. I remained in the woods in a tree across the deep hill between our house and the little church there until after dark. I was too scared to come home and after the crying stopped, I got lost into my pretend world where I was playing a game of hide and seek waiting to be found but knowing I had the best place ever. As the evening passed, I re-entered the real world and noticed that it was getting dark and as I slowly climbed down the tree, I felt the real pain that my world did not allow me to feel, I walked home slowly. When I finally did return he was waiting and informed me that I would not be eating for the next two days, and that I was to remain in the room during that time. At a very early age, the denial of food was a normal punishment and to minimize its affect I learned to do without. My mother would quietly sneak small morsels of food to me while I lay quietly and in pain on the hard floor with my single "cover" for two days. Food is irrelevant and a nonessential

part of my life yet my resolve to limit its
consumption may make it an essential cause
of my death.

CHAPTER 24

*How do you value life when you are not
valued, how do you establish morality when
no one around you has morals, how do you
show love when you don't know what it looks
like, what is sorrow and how and why does it
hurt?
You do it all by finding your value,
morals, love and sorrow in a book and then
mimic the actions of the characters, for
feeling does not exist only the stage:
lights, camera, ACTION!
-PGHG*

Hated

That was just the way he seemed to

release frustration. I and my siblings seem

to have been the source of much of his

frustration, thus suffering his wrath often.

"Strip down and line up" were the most

feared words we could here. We were ordered

to line up around the porch without clothing

(because I ain't beaten no clothes) and get

whooping's to make up for the times he

"knew" we had erred and did not get caught.

Living in fear was the only way we knew to

live. We were responsible for getting our own "switches" (tree branches commonly used in the south to discipline children for misbehavior) for the just-in-case beatings. Then one day we no longer had to get switches for Mr. Bruiser was born. Mr. Bruiser was a small three to four inches in diameter tree skinned and used as the beating bat of choice, and we were human balls and every hit was a homerun. My father was "Babe Ruth" he hit more homeruns on a single child than The Babe could have conceived.

By 1982 most of the work on the house was complete, there was now more room for my mother and fathers children and He added a trailer to the property. The trailer was added to make more living space for our extended and growing family. My father had many children and three wives. If everyone was home, which was very rare there were about nineteen children not including my siblings from Maryland who were not yet adults and often spent their summers wherever our father was. As children, we did not ponder the dynamics of the relationships but understood that nothing about our family was normal. Constant physical, sexual, and emotional abuse was the norm and without it, we were abnormal.

What is Normal?

The metaphysical dilemma that confounded our immature minds then and now was simply our purpose, the reason we were born. I believed I was unwanted by all who had any relative responsibility for my well-being; therefore, my rationale suggested that my existence was a mistake and I often tried to leave this life as to not continue to be a burden and an accident. I must say that fundamentally it sounds proper to state that there is a purpose for all and that no one is born without having a gift to leave this world however, what is fundamental about my life. Fundamental is defined as a basis of supporting the existence or determining the essential structure or function of a being. That being the case I am very sure that my essential purpose was to be a punching bag that sold to the highest bidder for the grand purpose of copulation. My gift was forced open long before my Christ-day, I never had a chance to know I had worth and I never will.

How can a gift be nurtured to give back when it was unwrapped and destroyed as a tissue used and discarded only to be recycled and used again. In a world that only provided the most abominable pain that could exist to humankind, I will never be anyone's gift, only a recycled and used tissue. Surely, it is clear that the type of nurturing I received will lead to despair for all who strive to embrace the victim of its wrath. Therefore, metaphysically speaking was it worth being born to experience the atrocities that were propagated at birth to morph into a being that can only bring continued pain to those who strive to love me.

CHAPTER 25

How do I explain what I cannot feel or what I do not understand?
-PGHG

The End

There was uneasiness around our home, my father was home less often and my mother was often with him, if she was not with him then my oldest sister was. The sirens coming down our road seemed constant and became the norm after some time had passed. It seemed to come more often and the ambulance would come into our yard, the drivers would get out, go into my sister's house to get my father, and take him away to the hospital. I had just turned eleven and did not understand anything that was happening; everything seemed out of order. We celebrated two Thanksgivings, two Christmases and they were the best we had ever had. My mother said, "just in case my

father was not alive for Thanksgiving and
later Christmas he wanted to make sure we
had good holidays." It seemed to me like he
was he trying to make up for the past hurts,
I knew he was sick, but not near death.

I did not know what death was and never
recall anyone dying before; therefore, I
could not truly understand what was
happening. In my mind, I was happy that he
was "dying." He was not mean anymore, and I
had been home for a whole year and four
months. I guessed I was home for good and we
would have no more beatings. I was in the
fifth grade and we were out of school for
the winter holidays when people started
regularly visiting our house. Soon after New
Year 1982, my father was in the bed in my
sister's trailer. He was brought home in an
ambulance. I did not see this because we
were back in school by then, but I would
learn my fate in it all and it was disguised

as opportunity in a tall stature in an unfamiliar place where I would be happy.

The smile on his face that morning was like none I remembered. I had never witnessed him in such a frail and humanly weak state only as a giant who was merciless. So, when called to him on this unforgettable morning and asked if I wanted to move with his sister to Florida; I sympathetically said yes. Observing his awkwardly weak frame and contorted features I was compelled by powers unbeknownst to me, to kiss him on the cheek and say "I love you." That was my first and only time of being close to him and feeling sorrow for him. He was weak and he asked so gingerly, as if he could not speak clearly the words that must be spoken to put things in order. I had never felt his skin before; it was soft and brown like the mahogany brown of beautiful furniture that you can only admire with a plastic cover protecting it from you. At the touch of my lips on his face he winced in agony that startled me and again made me see him as human. "Be careful that hurts." My father admitting pain, yes I see him in this rolling bed but I do not understand why and he is half the size he once was and what is a stroke and what does paralyzed mean? Who is man that resembles my father but is weak and frail and bound to this bed with wheels? What is wrong with him? I do not know the common terms I hear mentioned: lung cancer, stroke, paralyzed, a short time left. To do what, I wondered? I did not understand the agreement that I had consented to, "do you want to go to Florida with your my sister?"

As children, we did not understand the concept of disease or death, and parents provided little insight about the events that would follow the death of a parent. I had not lived at home long and the concept of leaving seemed normal. Florida was no more relevant to me than the grocery store, I had never been to either thus the magnitude of what leaving meant did not become clear until I was packed and in the car with my Aunt and my sister who was also sent to Florida by my father. I had never before met this woman who would play such a pivotal role in my life but this was not unusual because I had been at many homes to live with people that I had never met.

January of 1982 was a cold and somber winter for me. We the children were relegated to our rooms, which often led to fights and disagreements or sent to school only to return to an environment where there was little joy. It was after a weekend of fights my sister and I were asked about the Florida decision. Although there were five girls, my youngest sister was living with a

family in Greenville; and had resided with
them much of her life. My older sister was
grown and it was in her home a single wide
trailer that was on the property with our
home, where my father lay with half of his
body paralyzed dying from lung cancer left
untreated by his choosing. Therefore, with
my younger sister not at home, two of us
were on the road to the "the sunshine state"
and my older sister already grown with a
family, technically I have one sister
remaining at home with my mother.

Sent Away Forever

On January 26, 1982, we left for
Florida with my aunt, I did not know the
journey would be so long and was not sure
how long we would be visiting. I had only
been home for a short period of time when
this decision was made. I did not
understand the permanency of leaving but I
was compliant and simply behaved as an

obedient child given instruction would. I stayed in a child's place and ask no questions.

The ride was very long but I believed this would be different and maybe I had a chance. I ask no questions and did not converse, that is not what children do, they are to be "seen and not heard" I answered any questions that were asked but mostly, just rode quietly. I am sure that I fell asleep on the because it was a very long ride and for someone whose farthest distance was five hours to Georgia a couple of years earlier this trip was torture, but I dare not complain. I do not recall talking at all; even to my sister, I do not know if we stopped to eat or use the restroom, but I am sure that we arrived on the same day that we left; January 26 just late in the day. When I was awake I noticed beautiful big homes with yards that looked like they had perfect haircuts and adornments. Some had large front porches with swings on them and others had smaller porches with rocking chairs. I did not see people outside of these beautiful homes, just cars on the paved driveway, and fancy basketball goals that looked unused. I also saw many more homes that were like the ones I had lived in, broken porches, open doors for air, dirt yards, clothes on the line, and children playing with tree limbs for toys or running around just playing with each other. The car moved through larger cities and small towns; I remember seeing bridges with water under them that frightened me and large trucks that seemed too close, way too close to the car. All of these stimuli were being absorbed in my memory as conscious awareness and difference that made my little world of Mullins seem miniscule. I would imagine myself living in the large homes that had

perfectly groomed yards and basketball goals
sitting on paved driveways with fences
securing larger back yards.

I noticed that the farther we drove the
more congested the towns seem to become.
There were many mobile home parks and the
homes that did exist seem to be shacks or
old apartments but not in a community with a
name just on the streets. They were in close
proximity with tiny yards and little
walkways where one could walk beside or
behind a set of homes. People lived right
next to each other and they sat outside on
the steps of their home or stood on the
grass. I noticed that I did not see grocery
stores or shopping centers; but little
stores in the same area as the homes that
looked like former homes or really old gas
station stores. Many of the stores were in
places that I did not think a store could be
like in the middle of a street near the

trailer park, or just in an old dirt lot and people walked to them. Maybe, I was just not used to being out that much and what I thought was odd were actually normal.

In addition to the style of the homes, I also noticed that the people that were out seem to be aimless with no real purpose, just sitting on cars without shirts, or standing in a spot talking and smoking, and sometimes sitting on the porch. Where I had lived, most people seemed to work in the fields, factories, stores, schools, or somewhere every day. I did not know of anyone who just came out of their house to sit on the steps or on the porch for the day, yet it appeared to be common practice the longer we drove. This was all new to me and I felt closed and trapped into these small spaces that belonged to many people at once. The only separation was the small yards that connected one home to the other.

Why would anyone want to live this way? What did the children do if they could not go outside and play in the yard or what about Easter or summer Cookouts, had I been sentenced to jail?

Upon arrival to Jacksonville, Florida we went to my aunt's home, which did, have a small, front yard with a short wood fence around the whole yard including the larger back yard. One side of the house was narrow and kind of close to the neighbor's home but the other side was wider and was used regularly. Florida was different from any of the places we had driven through it was warmer in January than Mullins usually is and it had funny trees. The place where my aunt lived was a tall narrow kind of house, not like any houses I had lived. I had lived in one floor houses and houses with a room upstairs, but this house was different, it had rooms upstairs, downstairs and a place called a basement and had a front porch and back porch. The house was not made out of wood, and it wasn't brick, it was like rocks. Smooth rocks that were different colors like sandy, beige, orange and other muted earth tone colors. It had a three panel window on the ground level front that had Priscilla curtains and white blinds covering them. It had two regular windows on the top floor, and other windows that could be seen once we entered the house. The small front yard was filled to capacity with plants, rose bushes, hedges, and a variety of perennial plants that would bloom in a few months. It was obvious that my aunt enjoyed working in her small yard. There were chairs on the porch that provided a space to admire the beauty of the blooming plants and watch the cars drive by. I remember many days sitting with my aunt as she sang the old spiritual "Swing Low Sweet

Chariot Coming for to Carry Me Home." I loved those lazy spring and fall days when there was no cleaning, screaming, or hurt; just the thought of a chariot that would take me "home."

There were weekends when we went to St. Augustine or Atlantic Beach to shop for grocery and other items. She bought fresh vegetables, clothes, household products. We would also eat at the little deli's on those lazy fun Saturdays. I thought it was the most amazing thing to go into a restaurant and actually eat food that you order from a list of choices, and then people bring it to you, no cooking or washing dishes, just eating, paying and leaving. I had never experienced shopping or going out to eat or getting vegetables from a Market instead of the garden; for me this was worth cleaning up each Saturday and I wanted to do it perfect.

I was responsible for the untouchable museum room with all of the valuable "whatnots" that had to be handled gingerly and cleaned spotless "white glove tests spotless." I knew if it had been a good week and I did what I was supposed to, we would be setting out on a journey to one of the previously mentioned locations. Sometimes it was to purchase clothes for a special occasion and other times it was to get grocery or other food items especially fresh vegetables, but sometimes it was just to explore. My sensory glands were on high alert; I took in every sound and smell, and felt anything could be touched. These times I thought of my aunt as a kind person for taking my sister and me in when she did not have to.

I loved when we went to St. Augustine or to Atlantic Beach because there were "thousands" of stores and outside stands with fruit like oranges that I only had at Christmastime. They had what my aunt called grapefruit and I called "great fruit" and fresh fish that people would catch out of the biggest pond I had ever seen. They would catch them with different kind of fishing rods than the other lady I lived with and put them in boxes with ice and tops. I just could sit in the sun and soak in those free, painless moments forever. After returning to her house it was time to make Sunday dinner. It was better than any restaurant in the world to me; homemade everything—peach cobbler that had the most flaky, tasty crust imaginable. I truly had a fat tooth when she made special meals that also included yeast rolls that were amazing there were these little balls to the softest large pieces of dough that when placed in the oven would brown perfectly and quickly. With a watering mouth, I had to have one or two and if possible; I could have eaten them all.

In addition to going to the beach for the first time ever and enjoying the shopping experiences and the food, I felt special because I got to go to modeling school. I was given the opportunity to go to John Roberts Powers Modeling School in Orlando. I did not think I was pretty enough, old enough or skinny enough to model and I was short but it was all I could think about on the 2 hour drive and I really enjoyed the weekly classes. I had to be good to get to be able to have a ride each week, and if I was not nice I had to do other stuff. When I got there it was another world, I learned how to do a "pelvic tilt", walk straight with a crossover, how to walk and turn on the runway. I also learned etiquette and got to dress up in pretty clothes that were pretty to touch and made me feel pretty not dirty ugly or naked. My aunt was not perfect, but she was as close to perfect as I knew at that time. The price was not different than any other I had paid, but I did have the luxury of some opportunities that I had never before experienced.

In the back yard, she had a small vegetable garden that was nice to see (mostly because it was small). I had been in fields most of my life in Virginia and no garden was small the rows started in the east at the beginning of sunrise and did not seem to end until they met the setting of the sun in the west. Therefore, this little vegetable garden with green beans and tomatoes was almost humorous. In addition to a garden, she also had a clothesline, which would prove to be a near death sentence for my sister. Finally, there was a huge tree, which shaded the entire space that sat near the rear of the yard. It was a familiar space, nature existed there, and for me that was a piece of home.

Just inside the front entry was a path that led past several rooms all the way to the back of the house. The first room appeared to be a museum; all of the furniture was white with plastic covers and we were emphatically informed not to come into that room. It had what appeared to be thousands of little glass statues sitting on tables and stands. There was a large chest sitting on the west wall and the sofa sitting on the south wall making the room fill closed in and crowded. The large window was on the north wall and the entrance was from the east. On the chest sat pictures of family members that I would soon come to know and love. The chest was not just a chest it was an entertainment center that held records and a built in record player.

The center table had a doily on it with a glass vanity that held more of the glass statues. There were other special items that were not to be touched in the room and we were swiftly instructed not to enter it unless we were given permission. The wall behind the sofa was the stairwell that led upstairs and behind the stairwell was a large eat-in kitchen.

Traditionally arranged, the kitchen was not spectacular. It had linoleum floors unlike the living room that had hardwood floors. It had all of the normal cabinets, sinks and a table that was adorned with a tablecloth and salt and pepper shakers. Once in the kitchen I noticed another door and soon learned that it led to a basement. Past the kitchen was a back sitting room that seemed to be used for an anything room, it led to the backyard and had a curtain rather than a door to separate it from the kitchen.

After seeing the downstairs area, we were shown where our rooms would be upstairs. At the top of the staircase and to the right was my aunt's room, across the hall from her room was my sister's room and next to the bathroom (the only one in the house) was my room. I did not mind because my room had a window that looked out over the alley that led to the backyard and into the neighbors' backyard. There was a bed in my room and a small chest of drawers and I was fine with my space.

During our first week living with my aunt we were given a lot of rules about the house, and what we could and could not do, about our chores and informed of the trouble we would be in if we did not comply with the rules. We were also instructed on how she wanted her home maintained and that the expectations were not suggestions but edicts and laws punishable by the drop cord if not followed.

The Funeral

Within the week, my aunt received a call that my father had died on February 4, 1982, and before we could comprehend the words, we were in the car headed back to Mullins. I was very glad to be going home and excited to see my mother, brothers, and sisters. I did not like Florida therefore I was hoping I could finally just stay at home with my mother. Not understanding the limited concern that anyone had for my wishes, I was completely wrong and painfully hurt when reality set in. Not only could I not visit my mother when we arrived but I had to stay with my aunt at her sister's home and ride to the funeral with them while we were in Raynor, less than 15 miles from

Mullins but they would not let me go to see my mom.

It was as if I did not have a real family, like this was not my father and like my mother did not exist at all. Dazed and confused when my sister and I were allowed to go view my father's remains with my other older siblings I only remembered kissing my father's cheek and not uttering a word. I do not remember my mother being there and none of my brothers who lived at home were there only my mother's two oldest sons, my older sisters, and I. Where were my little brothers I thought? Why did I not get to go back home and be with my family instead of staying with relatives I barely knew? These thoughts were not verbalized and have honestly never been, for by the age of eleven, I already understood the ramifications of saying too much.

At the time I was not sure what I felt about my father's death; he had been a tyrant most of the time and did not seem to want me the rest of the time; therefore, while others cried at the viewing I sat stone-faced and quiet. The most vivid memory I have is the walk down the center church aisle to the front of a church like facility towards a dark colored box. The closer I came to the box the larger it seemed to become and about three quarters of the way I saw the side view of his face. I had never seen him asleep before or so still, and yet he appeared to be doing just that, sleeping. Dead had no meaning, so when I got to the box, it looked more like a bed, and he was lying on a white pillow with his legs lying under half of the box and a top waiting to be closed over his head. I looked at my father's face and could not resist touching his grayish toned skin and quickly jerked my hand back when I felt its coldness and how hard and stiff his skin felt. I stood a second longer and something urged me to kiss his cheek again, without being conscious of others in the room I numbly walked to a seat where my sisters sat and slid in beside them.

The only other memory of that period was watching the people come into the funeral. We all lined up in some predetermined order and as we walked into the small church, I noticed that there were people already inside. They were standing and watching as we entered and went to our seats. There were so many people there and I could not possibly know who they were or how they knew my father but it did not really matter; what did was the sheer number of people who attended this service. I watched the people inside and outside, just watched as the line of people coming in stretched on to eternity. My mother wore black and sat on the front row of the church with my older sisters and brothers and I was on the second row with more of them and other people I did not know. It was like watching a line of army ants returning to a red clay hill after a day of searching for food, it continued with splendid order and all people were quiet but I do not remember anyone crying as this procession continued. I do not recall anything else of the last day of seeing my father.

PART XIV

BY SOME ESTIMATES, HUNDREDS OF THOUSANDS
OF GIRLS AND BOYS ARE BOUGHT, SOLD OR
KIDNAPPED AND THEN FORCED TO HAVE SEX
WITH GROWN MEN

CHAPTER 26

It's about realizing, painfully, you've kept that voice inside yourself, locked away from even yourself. And you step back and see that your jailer has changed faces. You realize you've become your own jailer.
—Tori Amos

What's for Sale . . . Human Flesh

Upon returning to Florida, still unsure about what had happened and what it meant for me I simply got out of the car and walked in to the house on West Carter Street. I carried a small bag and as if in a daze, I walked up the stairwell and went into the place that had now been my sleeping quarters for a little more than a week. I vaguely remember commands being screamed out like, "get all of this mess out of the car and make sure it goes where it belongs," "don't leave those bags in the middle of the floor," and other commands that seemed to be nonsensical. I knew my father was no more alive because I saw his body in a big metal box, but it looked like his legs were cut off and he looked kind of ashen like he had been emptying the ashes out of the heater and they had gotten on his skin. He had a nice white shirt on that was clean, but his face and hands were ashy gray. I remembered when I kissed his cheek, I do not know why I did that but I did and he did not cry out in pain like he had a few weeks earlier when he asked me about this Florida place. There is a lot about that day that I do not remember, but what I will never understand is why I had to get back in the car and go away from my mother.

The screaming invaded my reflection of the past few days and caused me to become present and hear my aunt bellowing out commands at my sister and me. I felt like a zombie who had just awakened for the first time and did not know its purpose or its location. Mechanically, I managed to go through the array of commands and respond effectively. Of course, I learned this skill as a very young girl and learned to keep it as my best tool against confusion, pain, loneliness, and fear.

Long before my father died, he separated the girls from the boys. To me it was just after my brothers had raped me and I had learned to be quiet and not cry. Moving to the girls' room would seem like a great honor but I learned quickly that it only meant that now there was a price on my head. There were two beds, one of my sisters and I shared one and my other sister and half-sister from Maryland, the other. I remember vividly the night a person came into the side door and got into bed with my sister and they had sex and then he left her and moved to me. At nine or ten, I cannot recall my exact age, but I knew that I was to be quiet and just lay there. I noticed that a stream of boys or men, both were the same to me regularly followed this same process, at that time I just stayed quiet because we all knew what would happen if we talked about it even to each other and no one did. Although I did not understand how everybody knew to come to the side door, I did know that no one came on the property without my father's permission for anything. By the time he died, I had not been a virgin for several years and I was a mere eleven years old. I had not started my period yet and did not know what a period was, or contraception or sexually transmitted diseases; I was pretty ignorant. I do know that I never got to choose my first time and for anyone who has, or will cherish that choice.

I learned rather quickly after arriving in Florida, that sex was not only a lucrative asset to my father but to my aunt as well. She knew I was not pure, and after listening to my cousins angry remarks the Scarlet Letter must have been embroidered on my fifth grade head. I will never forget the first Sunday at Southern Baptist Church in Jacksonville. After returning home from my father's funeral, at morning service she said "the pastor wants to see you after church, just go right out the side door and his office is on the right." I thought he wanted to pray for me because my father had died or to say he was happy that I was there or maybe to give me "an encouraging word." Little did I know that what he wanted, he had bought, and that was me. The stain of my eleven years was seen through the clean clothes I wore that Sunday.

The reverend was very happy that I was there, so happy that he did not sit behind his big desk; oh no he moved his chair around to the front so that he could give me

some "words" and "lay on some hands." No
these words were not from the King James
Version of the Bible or any other version
that I am familiar with these words were
said clearly and slowly as his actions were
performed slowly and clearly.

  *"I just want you to understand that me
and your aunt have an agreement, and I will
have you (lifting my dress and pulling my
panties down to the floor) whenever I want
to and telling anyone will only get you into
trouble (looking closely into my tear filled
eyes, while putting his right index finger
and middle finger into my body). You see
this church belongs to me and what I want I
get, no one will believe you and I know you
are not new at this. When I suggest you ride
or come for you after school it would be
wise for you to be ready. Extension cords
are more painful than I will be. Now you
clean your face up and fix your clothes and*

go on out like a good girl, I will see you soon."

From that week forward, I was in his van, office or one of his deacons' offices who he shared me with to keep my mouth closed. I went against my better judgment and told my aunt who was vehemently angry with me for "spreading such lies because he was a man of God and I was a little liar spreading vicious rumors that could get me in trouble." The extension cord did hurt, and it left ugly bruises and marks that were grotesquely painful without being touched. The pain was terrible but the embarrassment of the marks were far worse, I was used to beatings with switches, sticks, boots, fists but the extension cord was very different which meant that even in the summer I had to wear my arms and legs covered after a beating so that no one would see the whelps. I refused to let anyone hug or touch me.

I belonged to the preacher from 1982 to 1984 (fifth, sixth, and seventh grades) and again, from 1988 to 1989 (eleventh and twelfth grades). Although I told others and even asked my sister if he had touched her (he had not) nothing changed. When I was younger I had the privilege of going to modeling school and learned proper etiquette, this was very useful when I went to the prom with his son as I was instructed. His daughter was my friend and I was a member of the youth choir where we travelled regularly to sing at churches in other states, but I could not tell them, they would have only one of two outcomes. The first possibility would be that they believe me, and I destroy their family and they hate me for existing, or second they do not believe me and hate me for lying on their father. I knew the end of this story and chose to keep my mouth closed and do as I was told.

On many of those out of town church trips I would have to take the detour and fulfill his wants, or evenings after school he would be waiting and drive to an empty parking lot, a wooded space, or Friendship Park. He could go anywhere because he was a preacher and had a big blue van with dark windows, and he proved how easy it was because even when the places had many people no one ever worried about the light and dark blue Chevrolet van. He did what he wanted, I cried and asked him not to get me pregnant and he said not to worry because he had a vasectomy so that was not a problem. I remember his strange tools and the way he used them to help him be "happy," I was required to do stuff that I never knew existed and feel pain from acts like oral and anal sex. I remember how he hurt me, and how my silent tears bought no mercy or compassion. I think he worked at some kind of construction or cement company because he always smelled like sand or dirt after rain; I will never forget that smell. I was isolated and alone with the craziness, yet it was not new to me. By my senior year, I had decided that there was nothing left to fight for therefore what was the point in living. I never expected or desired to get married or to get to thirty years of age, I always prayed to die and that did not change for a long time.

I close my eyes and I write about you, I write about your touch, your smell, your tone, your breath. You are with me at all times. I try to put you out of my mind and yet the fear that you illicit draws me in and requires me to fall at your feet. I am afraid of your glaring eyes, and when they are closed I see them; large, angry, and piercing my very core. I know that if I move or speak you will quickly open them and they will meet my face only seconds before your large fists close my eye. I hear myself scream, yet I cannot understand why. Why can I not get used to your touch, why does my heart beat drown out my thoughts when I know your near, I am familiar, but I remain afraid. You are no more, but when I close my eyes I smell you and hear you and I am afraid.

CHAPTER 27

*Sometimes when I'm alone, I cry because
I'm on my own,
All the tears I cry are bitter and
warm; they flow with life, and take no form.
Ah, the world moves fast and it would
rather pass you on by than to stop and see
what makes you cry
It's painful, so sad, sometimes I cry."
—Tupac Shakur*

Wanting Home—Home not Wanting Me

After the seventh grade I returned to
Virginia hoping to be embraced and welcomed
with open arms. Not quite, I was an
inconvenience to my mother who had moved
into a relatively new three bedroom
singlewide mobile home. My younger brother
had one of the rooms and the other was empty
of human habitation, it was primarily a
neatly kept storage space. Therefore, I
slept on the sofa bed for a while and
eventually was moved into the room on a twin
bed.

My short stint at home was the summer before the eighth grade in school and through the completion of the ninth grade. The visit was so short and a visit in the truest since after a fight that my mother gave the win to my half-brother. An unexpected visit from my half-brother changed everything. He came to Virginia from Washington D.C. for a visit at the beginning of the summer after I completed the ninth grade, he was given my borrowed space and I was placed back on the sofa bed in the living room. One hot summer night while asleep, I felt the familiar creeping in the night and awoke to my brother, who had to be twenty-five or thirty years old at the time, removing the covers and my panties simultaneously. I lay quiet in the fetal position because I felt I would be safe this time. I believed that because I was menstruating, he would not continue this endeavor, but again I was mistaken, he pried my legs with the intent of going forward. I screamed out! I expected him to leave, but he did not budge, I jumped up and screamed. Finally, my mother came into the living room and asked what was going on and I quickly stated that he was trying to rape me? He did not deny anything just innocently looked at my mother and said, "Well I guess I'll go on to bed now." My mother in her usual frustrated tone for being awakened simply said, "I think you should." Each left the room with me looking and feeling obsolete.

PART XV

LIFE IS NOT WORTH LIVING IF YOU HAVE TO
LIVE LIKE ALLISON. I WAS STRIPPED OF MY
SOUL, LOVE, FAITH, BODY, MY CHANCE FOR
A NORMAL LIFE ALL BECAUSE I MESSED UP
WHEN I WAS FOUR AND I DID NOT MEAN TO,
BUT NO ONE WILL EVER BELIEVE ME.

CHAPTER 28

*We endure so much more than we think we can,
all human experience testifies to that. All
we need to do is learn not to be afraid of
the pain. Grit your teeth and let it hurt.
Don't deny it, don't be overwhelmed by it.
It will not last forever. One day the pain
will be gone and you'll still be here.*
—Harold Kushner

Gaddi on the Move

After that, I ran away and went to
Baltimore for the remainder of the summer
and through the winter of my tenth grade
year in school. Initially, I was just there,
I spent a few nights at my sister's
apartment and some at their mother's and
wherever I was welcome. While there, I lived
with one of my brothers and his wife and two
young children. Of course, I was an
inconvenience but I had always been and knew
that would never change.

Unfortunately, school was quite
different. I cannot tell you what the name

of the high school was and there are no
records of my attendance, but I started the
tenth grade there and was shocked by the way
students behaved. I remember sitting in my
science class on the front row waiting for
the rotund clean faced white as snow male
teacher to begin his lesson, but all he did
was ignore the spitballs, chewing gum, card
games, and other disruptive class behaviors
as if they were not taking place. It was as
if I had walked into the school for juvenile
offenders that were not policed.

Living so close to the school meant
that I could walk home or ride the bus, and
I would do both with no particular reasoning
for doing one or the other. I walked with a
group of "friends" home one day about a
month after beginning. The girl was actually
my "friend" and I did not know the guys at
all. As we got close to her home she asked
if I wanted to stop by for a little bit and

watch television. Of course, I wanted to; I would rather do anything than go to that house and be in trouble, when we entered the house it was quiet and the only lights were from the windows all four of us went into the living room and she turned on the television. I remember us being silly; I do not remember when my friend left the room because I was playing with her "boyfriends" friend. At first, it was just simple throwing the throw pillows and seeing who could hit the other, and then it was actually hitting one another with the pillows, before I realized what was actually happening I was in a terrible position. He was tickling me, and tickling me and I was laughing and "having fun" then I realized he was touching me on my breasts, and taking my shirt off and still tickling me. I started fighting him off vigorously and he restrained me but could not continue to take my clothes off at the same time so when he would let go of my hands, I would fight for my life, kick, and scream, but no one came. Eventually, with torn clothes and bruises I was able to get up and run out without being raped. I looked horrible, went in the house through a side entrance, and quickly went upstairs to get myself cleaned up. I never told anyone and never went back to that school.

Again, I ran away. Not from Baltimore, just from that brother's house and went to stay with my sister in the projects. It was scary there but I used her identification and enrolled in another school. I did not stay anywhere long, I went to school sometimes, but it was not a priority. Some nights I would stay with their mother. After a while I just stayed on the streets, it was summer and no one wanted me to make their home mine. I met another girl who was my age 15 or 16 and she had no home either. Therefore, we stayed together and would just walk around during the day and find a semi safe place at night.

CHAPTER 29

Some people are afraid of what they
might find if they try to analyze themselves
too much, but you have to crawl into your
wounds to discover where your fears are.
Once the bleeding starts, the cleansing can
begin.
—Tori Amos

This is a scary place where memory is
fragmented and even today I cannot make
sense of exactly how everything happened. I
have not asked much of the readers until
now. I ask for your understanding as I try
to bring this terrible time to surface. I
try to remember and analyze how it all
happened but the miasma that blocks my
clarity is so thick that I need a little
compassion for the broken parts of this
recollection.

Photographs of Chains

One evening while sitting outside on
the stoop in front of an abandoned house we
were asked by a clean cut man if we wanted

something to eat, we thought about it for a few minutes before answering. We rationalized, what harm could it be for two very hungry girls to walk to McDonald's and get something to eat. We knew that we should not have gone but days of no real food was enough to blind rational minds and our stomachs made the decision for us. We went with him to McDonald's where he purchased our meals and one for himself. Everything was cool, we talked and there were no cues to make us question his motives. He told us he lived down the street and was a photographer and because we were both "pretty girls," he would like to take our pictures if we did not mind. He was never aggressive or desperate; his kind demeanor and our need for self-efficacy clouded our judgment. She was Puerto Rican and I am Black but we looked very similar, caramel colored skin curly hair and small bodies.

We eagerly agreed, rationalizing at the intelligent age of fifteen that taking pictures was harmless and we might get famous so what could taking a picture hurt? We went smiling down the street as we arrived at what appeared to be a normal Baltimore row house on an average street. When we entered, it had gray carpet and was spacious, but had very little furniture. The room had a photo stand with a camera attached a wooden bar stool that sat behind the camera and stand and a couple of twin sized mattresses beside each other on the floor. He apologized for the limited furniture and said that he had just moved in and had not fully settled yet; we believed him and told him it was okay.

My friend and I were not fresh; and we knew we looked too filthy to take pictures. All three of us sat on the floor and ate our meals as he made what seemed to be small talk. He asked where we lived and what time did we have to be home. We stupidly answered the questions by telling him that we had met down the street and was just trying to find a place to stay for a while. The small talk continued and we drank our beverages and ate our meals without any apprehensions. We asked him what kind of pictures he took and he provided us with an answer that we swallowed just like we did the food.

I do not know how long we were asleep or when we were moved but when we awoke we were not in the same place that we fell asleep. I was undressed and my friend was not next to me. I tried to move and realized that I was bound to the feet of a radiator naked but with many more mattresses. I groggily woke looking for my friend who was not beside me and then I realized my state. I tried to scream but my mouth was taped shut, I tried to free my hands but that too was a futile effort. Then I scanned the room and realized that I was not alone. There were many girls who appeared to be around my age and were in my same state, they watched as I became lucid and noticed the fear in my eyes as the tears rolled down my face. No one said a word even though they had no tape on their mouths. After a few minutes, a man that I had never seen before, an older man came close to me and informed me that I would be there a while and that I had two options. Do as I am told like a good girl, or do what I am told by force; it was my choice. Because I could not speak, I just looked at him through tear filled eyes as he ran his hands over my body and acknowledged that it was good, and should bring in a good price.

CHAPTER 30

*I've been crawling up so long on your
stairway to heaven
And now I no longer believe that I wanna get
in
And will there always be concerts where
women are raped
watch me make up my mind instead of my face.*
—Sleater Kinney

Expectations without Questions

Once again, I was the captured one in this web of life. I fought for the first few months and after being forcibly drugged, beaten, repeatedly raped by men who just seem to come and go, I was starved and eventually I had no more tears and no more fight. I became docile and obedient, I would smile and whisper kind words to those who paid to be with me, and I would comply with every command. I learned how to live without food much earlier under my father's tutelage. I had been anorexic for years, thanks to my father's punishment for misbehaving; therefore, I just dissociated and decided to accept my hell. I had never been drugged and it took very little for me to become completely oblivious to what was happening to me or who was doing it. I did not know one drug from another some were injected, others were force-fed, but they all were effective. After I stopped fighting, I became a "good" candidate. After remaining docile for several months, I was informed that I was ready to move up. I did not know what "moving up" meant, I thought I would be given food regularly and some real clothes because I had seen other girls leave and they did not come back to the warehouse room with beds and chains. I misunderstood what the conditions were. I was taken off the mattress and into another room, where there were clothes, not just any clothes, but clothes like models would wear. I was dressed in a very revealing red and black outfit similar to the one the photographer had, and informed that I would be taken to a location where I could make a lot of money if I was "good" and could make the men happy. I was told that I would be given to wealthier men who paid more and I had to be really sexy and do whatever they wanted. I was warned to always secure the money before I had sex and make sure to have it all when I was picked up, and not to try anything or I would be killed. The instructions were clear and Leila was in charge. She knew what to do, how to walk, talk and smile so that the men were happy. She was great, and always made money.

After a few weeks when it appeared that trust had been earned, I remember the night that Gaddi took the lead. I stood in the spot not very far from the Harbor and after only a brief moment a car pulled up and I approached it and asked if I could do anything for the man inside. He looked at me with eyes that were hungry, and said yes and get in quick. I got into his car and was driven to a dark alley where I got the money I was told to ask for, $150.00, and then proceeded to make the man happy. When I was done, I got out of the car in the alley instead of letting him take me back to the meeting spot. I took off my shoes and ran to the first bus I saw and asked how to get to the Greyhound Bus Station. Dressed in virtually nothing it was obvious that I was a whore, fortunately, I was already in the general area and the driver went two blocks south of where I had gotten on the bus and dropped me off with directions.

I bought a one-way ticket to Virginia and sat there afraid that I would be caught. Once on the bus I sat near the front in an open seat beside a man. Once we left, I leaned on the window and began drifting off to sleep. I felt the man's hands touching me, he began by rubbing my arm, then my side and proceeded to touch other parts of my body. I knew how I was dressed and felt that there was no point in saying anything. Leila took over and he enjoyed himself. When the bus arrived in Washington DC, I changed buses for the Virginia bus that would not arrive for another hour. To avoid the noticeable and understandable glares, I went into the restroom and remained until I heard that the bus was loading. I found an old shirt in the bathroom, although it was soiled, it was better than the nothing that I had on. The next seven hours I slept, and stayed very distant from anyone.

CHAPTER 31

These are our demands:
We want control of our bodies.
Decisions will now be ours.
You can carry out your noble actions,
We will carry our noble scars.
Reclaimation.
No one here is asking,
No one here is asking,
But there is a question of trust.
You will do what looks good to you on paper,
We will do what we must.
Return, return, return.
Carry my body."
—"Reclamation" by Fugazi

News Spreads Fast

Again, I had runaway. I came home to the unwelcoming hands of my mother who did not have room for me so I asked my sister if I could stay with her. They lived on the same property that my father had purchased prior to his death, just on opposite sides of the yard. My sister did not mind at all and let me sleep in her young daughter's room. I enjoyed being there; I was with my family again and started school back in

March of my tenth grade at Barter High
School.

They had all seen the story on the news
and yet did not know that I was one of the
captured girls. However, they did know that
I had taken pictures without clothes. The
images had been sent everywhere, including
my small southern town and when I arrived,
it was no secret what was thought of me; and
I would prove to pay because of the
implications. I heard the rumors and the
names and knew what my peers thought of me.

I kept to myself and tried not to
become friends with anyone. I was considered
weird for many reasons; therefore, I would
not talk to many people. I was smart, most
of the people in my classes were white, and
therefore I was a loner. I had two friends,
I felt comfortable around them and would
visit their homes and really have an
amazingly fun time.

I would periodically get calls from the man who held me captive and he would threaten to come find me and kill me. I do not know how he found the telephone number to my sister's house but he did and I would listen and pretend that everything was fine. Again, I learned early in life that telling only made things worse. Honestly, I expect the same thing by doing so now. I am afraid of the consequences, but I cannot keep it inside anymore.

I worked at the chicken restaurant that summer before my eleventh grade year and thoroughly enjoyed it, I would by a few clothes from the Salvation Army and maybe even from K-Mart if I had a little extra which was not often. My junior year of high school, the calls had simmered and I had become less afraid of being killed and was a bit spryer in my junior year. This led to unwanted attention.

School, Not So Good

I had more than my share of advances, most I could just say no and they understood, others not so much. I was on the track team and jumped 100 and 300-meter hurdles (not fast) and I was a "mat maid" for the wrestling team with a group of girls. During wrestling season, we were responsible for cleaning the area and sweeping the floor and putting up the mats. I was always the last to leave because I waited for my sister to get off work at 5:00 PM and drive from Lancing to the school, which was usually never a problem.

However, one unwanted pursuer, a big guy on campus both in size and intimidation, had been making advances for a while and had obviously gotten tired of me ignoring him. After the other team left and the coaches, many of the students lived close by and hung around after the meets. The gym was under the cafeteria and had glass windows all around its perimeter. I came from the back with the broom in my hand and heard him tell everyone to get out of the gym. When I came around the corner he punched me and took the broom out of my hands, kicked me as he cursed me for "thinking I was too good for him." Outside the windows were ablaze with people watching and no one helping. He tore off my clothes and proceeded to rape me in front of a large number of students who just stood by and watched. When he finished, I ran out of the wrestling room to the girls' locker room where he followed and slapped me again. I cried and fell to the floor until he left. It seemed to be an eternity. Then I put on my gym clothes that stayed in my locker, washed my face and did not leave the locker room until I knew my sister had arrived. I never said a word; and I never returned to that school.

CHAPTER 32

*Most men fear getting laughed at or
humiliated by a romantic prospect
while most women fear rape and death.*
—Gavin de Becker

Preachers, Deacons, and Brother

I returned to Florida the next day by
hitchhiking and begged my aunt to let me
stay at her house. By now, she was married
or getting married soon and was not living
in the house that we moved to when we went
to Florida. First, she let me know that not
only would I pay her $500.00 per month, and
that I had not completed my part of the
agreement she had with the preacher and if I
planned to stay there those were the
conditions. He was very ready to have me
under him again, and as punishment, I was
shared with one of the deacons, and others
who he influenced. I shrugged my shoulders
because by this point what difference does

it make. I was forced to go with his son who I really liked, to the prom. I loved the prom, but I really liked his son but could not date him for obvious reasons. Although, I liked him being in a relationship with him was not possible, I just had to follow instructions, I was his father's property.

I prayed every night to die and death would not come. After being forcibly drugged in Baltimore I was afraid to take medicine and I have never touched a gun, and hanging seemed painful, so I just wanted God to take me out of my misery. I did not know why this was my life. I was always calm, smart, and tried to be a good person who would not harm anyone and yet my life was full of pain. I do not know how much was my fault and how much was my destiny in life, but what I knew was that I just wanted something better or death, which at the time seemed better.

HOW DID I GET HERE?

CHAPTER 33

It already is bigger than everything else. It lives in front of me, behind me, next to me, inside me every single day. My schedule is dictated by it, my habits by it, my music by it.
—Daisy Whitney

Mother

I do not know her and she does not know me. She never wanted to be a part of my life and refused my attempts to return home. Maybe I was confused to think that I had a home and she was my mother, I think she was my entry into earth but never my mother. She says "Allison I don't know why your father did not let you stay home, all I know is that he said he was taking you somewhere." I asked "What did you do, did you try to stop him, and why me" she says "you know how your father was". No more no less, no regrets she has no remorse and yet I yearn for her love. She is lost in denial and has a clean heart in her mind. I do not just mean physically lost but also emotionally oblivious to the pain of her seed. This is true, for how could you say "stop that crying and clean up her face, cause that's just the way life is, it won't be the last time so get cleaned up and get back outside and go play." Back then and now I struggle with those instructions the nightmares of the experience and all the experiences that followed seem to control my forward mobility. I feel stunted in a world of trying to recapture my stolen self so that I can take off the mask forever. I am the quintessential hamster running in circles, when everyone says there is no point, forget it, stop living in the past and move on, I run, seeing much of the same scenes awake and in sleep.

I am the kind of human that needs an answer and I do not know who I am and no one else seems to know. All I have is the one who brought me into this world and she will not answer. Not long after I had my first daughter at 19, got married at 21 and my second daughter at 23, a hatred that I could not hide reared its head for my mother. As a mother, I cannot imagine anyone taking, harming, or sexually abusing my girls, I felt such a deep bond with them that I felt I would murder anyone that hurt my girls. My husband, stated in a most concerned voice "why don't you just ask her again; ask her why did she let so many things happen to you and why she did not bring you home." It sounded like the simplest thing in the world, but I physically panicked, I became overwhelmed with anxiety and terrified of the truth. I knew what I wanted to hear, "I am sorry, I have always loved you, and wanted you with me, I have no excuse, but I will be here if you want from now on" that was my idealism. I could not imagine talking to her about the past and hearing "well, that's just the way things were" in her nonchalant passive voice. Talking to my mother was difficult, she is not a conversational person but more of what is commonly called in many black churches as a "call and response" communicator she answers or responds to direct questions without elaboration or emotion, which is difficult if the right question is not explicitly asked. If it is she responds with the off-handed remark of "well you know how…was". She does not offer terms of endearment such as "I'm happy to see you," "I love you," or actions (hugs) without first receiving that which you want. If I want a hug, I must go to her with arms outstretched, and she will respond, if I say I Love You, she will repeat, she does not initiate affection. Therefore, my very real fear of being dismissed with one of her responses was initially prevented me from asking any questions.

However, I could not overcome my need to know therefore I fought my fears because I wanted to ask her many questions: "Why did you let me be raped by my brothers?" "Why did you give me away?" "Why did you not want me?" Why did my name not get added to my birth certificate until I was five?" And most importantly, "Are you my real mother?" Now that I was a mother, I could not imagine departing with my daughter; her beautiful innocence needed total protection and even more love than I could have ever imagined and this made my mother's decisions to have no rational meaning to me. The possibility of hearing her voice a response made my heart pound at a rate that was utterly terrifying; I physically thought I was having a heart attack. I was paralyzed with fear but fear had never stopped me from taking a step into the unknown before to find the answers and it did not this time.

I decided to go to my mother's home and asked her to ride out with me to talk for a while; we had a respectful relationship so she had no problem with the request. Once in the car I in my natural nature immediately asked the questions that had been burning my spirit and taking my life. All of the questions were asked as tears blinded my vision of the road in front of me. I remember having to pull to the side of the road because I could not see clearly enough to drive safely. After asking all of the questions and observing my emotional instability my mother simply stated, "Well you know how your father was and how things were back then." I did not know or understand her answer and broke the questions down into individual questions, like "Why did you let my brothers rape me and tell me to clean my face and go outside and play?" "That was just the way things were, your father was just that kind of person." "What about my name being added to my birth certificate in 1975, five years after I was born?" "That dumb hospital you know how they did things back then?" "But my brother who is eleven months older and the one who is seventeen months younger all born at the same hospital had theirs signed." "Well I don't know what that doctor was thinking." "What about giving me away?" Again, "That was your father, I would get so mad when I would see people come and he would just take my girls and give them away, I couldn't do anything." Shut down! When the questions continued and eventually my mother completely shut down and her tone changed and agitated she stated, "That's just how your father was and I didn't have anything

to do with what he did." That was it, from
1991, when I asked those questions until
today the answers have been the same
noncommittal, unemotional answers that I
received at seven years old basically, suck
it up, and get over it already.

PART XVI

THE JOURNEY IS DIFFICULT, AND YET I
KEEP LOOKING, I WANT TO KNOW WHO I AM
AND MAYBE I AM JUST A CHILD OF GOD AND
THAT MUST BE ENOUGH~

CHAPTER 34

The journey continues, but now I have just
found the exit sign. I have been blindly
walking through this jungle where the
branches slap my face and the animals rip
the skin from my bones trying to reach my
soul, now badgered, bruised and tired I find
exit gate and it is open.
                    -PGHG

Revelation

The day had come when all would be

revealed; so I thought. Not just the incest

the rapes, or the prostitution but the names

of the perpetrators. Twenty years had passed

and many ventures had been tried to mask the

hurt the loss and most importantly the

stains of filth and worthlessness that

dictated my every action. Promiscuity,

anorexia, running away from struggle and

fear, were my coping skills. I would quickly

clear away the tears that came from the pain

and push them into the overflowing place

deep in my heart; my Black's Box to avoid

dealing or thinking about the realities of what my life really was. Yet every move was in search of what was missing; a gentle touch, a loving arm, a kind word, an embrace that was without strings attached, and most importantly, a validation that I, Allie Hampton, was worth more than the dust of the earth.

Yet today I am here alone in this place called home; paralyzed from the memories that hinder me from remaining gainfully employed in the areas of employment where I could be most effective because they become triggers and cause terrible restlessness, disassociation, nightmares, and acts of the past. I take Prozac to help me to have a good mood and Klonopin to prevent me from being overcome by anxiety. The thing I want the most in this world I come to realize that I may never obtain—answers. I thought my life was working and that I was strong and fine for the past twenty years I have been able to marry the best man in the world and remain in the marriage happily, bring two wonderful children from birth to adulthood with solid values and drive, and even achieve the highest level of education available. It all sounds great until it all ended. Yes, I am still married to the great man given to me by God and his love is without condition, and yes, I do have two great beautiful independent educated daughters, and yes, I have all the education the world suggests; yet I have no idea who I am without being mommy or a student, or having to prepare dinner.

Therefore, I set out on a mission to find out who I am and how I arrived at this point. With very little knowledge about who and where I have been and what transpired on my journey. I remembered pieces as if my life was a shattered glass with hundreds of glaring pieces just waiting to get in your foot and cause excruciating pain. The larger pieces were easier to manage, but those fine glimmers that remained unrevealed except after lots of questions and many tears and often no answers, those are the ones that cut deeply and cause pain that goes unchanged. I know you must ask what is so devastating that you continue to allude to the mysteries but never reveal them. I must ask for your patience because you have had the great privilege of reading much of the surface pieces of my story as I was learning them so now I need your patience to reflect on the depth of Allie. You see from this point forward you will see what I saw as I lived it.

CHAPTER 34

*And God shall wipe away all tears from
their eyes; and there shall be no more
death, neither sorrow, nor crying, neither
shall there be any more pain: for the former
things are passed away.*
—Revelations 21:4

Unfortunately, the hope lies in
reliving the terrors and recognizing that
they are not present now. But when I close
my eyes, the movies play over and over in my
head. When I watch television if someone is
hurt, I am hurt. I do not like large crowds
for people touch me that I do not know and I
am afraid. I refuse to go around too many
family members because I am not like them, I
cannot get over it, I cannot make my head
shut off. I try not to feel for if I do I
will be in trouble, tears are not allowed
and who cares, no one. I put on a huge smile
so that no one asks what is wrong. I cannot
do poorly everything has to be perfect. I am

tired but rest will not come, for when I
close my eyes the movie plays again and
again. I awake not knowing my location; I
awake afraid trying to escape. I have awaken
outside, I have awaken fully unclothed and
with no memory as to why.

You see when I am afraid, or nervous or
unsure; I fall into a character a child, the
sexually promiscuous child, the terrified
hide in the closet child, or the stand in
front of 500 people and speak with authority
professional who leaves not remembering any
of the actions of any of the characters.
Thank you in advance for your empathy, but
now I must say that my greatest fight is to
learn how to feel that empathy, because I
know how to separate what happens from any
feelings; love, pain, tears, hate, anger,
and even passion were all let go a long time
ago and weekly I sit in therapy embarrassed
when the tears come, but yet cannot

understand why being anorexic is so bad. I feel fine, yes fine, drugs will do that for you, but it seems that everyone else has an issue with me going from 172 lbs to 119 lbs in a span of four months. I hurt so deeply that I must take the pain away, not by cutting or committing suicide, but food is not a necessity, and running miles takes the pain from my mind and places it in my physical body. So maybe when you all help me not to feel so scared to publicly feel all of your eyes on me; hopefully not seeing me as less than the dirt and only as dust, maybe then I can look in the mirror and see someone worth loving. I am afraid of what is in these many years of journals and this portion of the book is not from memory, it is real time and it has taken me months to find strength to put them out for judgment. Many of the journal writings clearly reveal several of the personalities and often seem irrational, some may have no relationship and almost all will be in the voice of the part of me that is in pain. Leila, Gaddi, Laural, Professional Intellectual, or the worst but most revealed identity who protects me from terror is revealed through rebellion, pride, and arrogance.

CHAPTER 35

*The thief cometh not, but for to steal,
and to kill, and to destroy: I am come that
they might have life, and that they might
have it more abundantly.*
—John 10:10

Finding Something to Believe In

Jesus Christ has been and continues to be my only redeeming feature. Every time I ran away or was being victimized, I prayed. Yes, as the title suggests I prayed to die, for me I meant a literal death and thus tried many times. However, God had and has a different plan for my life; he killed many things when I asked for death and now one of the most obvious deaths was my memory. God took the most dreadful memories away. One may say that the life I have led has been dreadful and what could be worse than what is shared? Each week I attend therapy angry because I cannot remember portions of my life that are just cut off, they do not come to me, I cannot put the pieces together. I have secured every possible document from health records to school records but neither fill in the blanks, birth certificate is of no help and I have no one who has been with me that can fill in the blanks. Therefore, I must say he answered my prayers and killed the parts of my life that would have possibly led me to drugs or other escaping tactics that could have literally taken my life. Now full of frustration and anger I fret because I have no pictures, memories or people of my youth to tell me what kind of person I was.

In all of this I made it a point to cherish my girls and make sure there were and are many pictures, that they had stability, and never questioned if they were loved. At nineteen when I wanted life to end and my daughter was two months old, my life began. I gave up and the third Saturday in August after nights of terror and days of hearing voices, I ignorantly gave God an ultimatum. "God tomorrow I am going to church and you know I do not believe in any preacher but I am going to give you a chance to fix me, and if you don't fix my life tomorrow I will come home and kill myself, I can't take it anymore, I give up." On the third Sunday in August, I entered the church my mother and other relatives attended; sat near the rear with my daughter in my arms and did nothing. At some point in the service, I heard the preacher say, "If anyone wants Jesus to be their Lord and Savior you can come now." I did not move I just sat there until someone behind me tapped my shoulder and said, "You told me you would give me a chance, now go." I looked beside me and behind me and no one was there, but without additional thought I rose and went to the front of the church where others were, I held my daughter close

and just stood there. I did not know what to
do until a woman whispered and said pray for
what you want. Someone took my child (I do
not remember who or when but I did not have
her so someone had to take her out of my
arms). I had never prayed in front of people
and really did not know how to pray. I knew
the prayer in Matthew chapter 6, but that is
not what I wanted. Again she said just close
your eyes and talk to Jesus. I did as I was
instructed and slowly began to talk to God
as if he was standing beside me or in my
head. I told him everything I could and I
apologized for my life and asked him to fix
me; I did not know about salvation or a Holy
Ghost, I just needed something greater than
me to believe in. I explained that for
nineteen years, my life was not worth living
and that one day I wanted to be happy and
not hurt to my core. I realized that I was
crying an ocean of salty tears that even

today become uncontrollable because he gave me a new life at that moment. I knew because although I physically did not look different I felt a releasing that seemed to weigh tons come from my body and what entered was strange to me; hope what was that. I had never believed or wanted a tomorrow and now I, Allie, have hope and faith. It could not have been anything but God for it has kept me safe and unhurt for twenty-two years. After being raped, sodomized and molested for years by a preacher, God still loved me enough to give me salvation. I know that for some, I am less than the soil on the bottom of their shoes but for some reason on that day, twenty-two years ago, Jesus thought I was worth a chance.

Life has not been easy but within a month, he sent me a friend I had never met, but we have never parted since October 7, 1990. He legally adopted my daughter before she was a year with the blessing of her wonderful father who came from Philly to make sure he and his family was solid. We married March 7, 1992 and after two losses, he blessed us with another daughter in 1994. Both girls are amazing young women who have accomplished great honors in their own right. Full of life, energy and extremely well adjusted and happy with themselves and life. My friend and my husband is indescribable, he makes me laugh, he is so extremely intelligent till it is scary and yet he is gentle and loves me. A degree in Computer Science is a mask for his true passion of History and Comedy. I only asked for one thing from him the first day we met and that was for him to one day make me laugh from my soul. He promised he would and that it would not be for only one day but many days and twenty-three years later, I continue to have gut wrenching laughs from the greatest man on earth for me. God has blessed me to be surrounded by people who care, and although I am afraid to let people get close, he takes great care to ensure that I am safe.

I share my story often to youth and adults alike who need to know that it does not matter where you start just that you keep moving and seek direction from something greater than humankind. Understanding that humans are fallible thus unreliable, my Lord and Savior Jesus Christ made it possible for me to go from having no name to having some respect not greater than anyone. Possibly, without Jesus, I am greater than no one with him I am an heir to his throne and my faith is not centered in a church for I do not attend a church regularly for many things are said that exclude the principles of Jesus but benefit the greed of man. I may be wrong but again I put my faith, trust and resources in the hands of God who directs me into all truth and righteousness according to his plan for Allie's life.

It is my prayer that my story will help someone to believe that there is hope even for you. God loves me no more than he loves you, and he even understands my aversion to church but does not leave me because my life is his. Not like the scribes and Pharisees where only actions were relevant but like the woman that had done much wrong and Jesus in his wisdom told her to go and sin no more after forcing the stone throwers to judge themselves first. Or like the thief on the cross that simply said "Lord forgive me . . . ." And Jesus without question did. He has not given his power to humans to dole out we can go to him and he is the only one who can heal, cleanse and purify our souls and make our broken pieces seamless without cracks.

To Allie with Love

Made in the USA
Charleston, SC
05 June 2014